If you would enter Philippe's gallery be prepared.
Leave your certainties and preconceptions in the
foyer.
Do not be deceived by the jovial host, the armchair
and the reference books.
You are about to undertake a voyage of visual
exploration.
Be willing to adjust your lenses from magnified to
macro.
As you wander though the labyrinth of canvases, you
will find yourself at the hub of a kaleidoscope.
Here you will find beauty and artistry arising out of
processes.
Watch, as simple colours merge, mingle and melt
into opaque and vitreous streams.
Don't fish for the familiar.
The artist, the arbiter, has stripped away all
superficialities to bring you the inner spaces
Of natural and celestial forms.
There are placid pools of tone along the way.
Yet even there you might feel undercurrents of
mutation.
When you leave, your exhilaration will make the
outside world a richer place.

Pat Brock

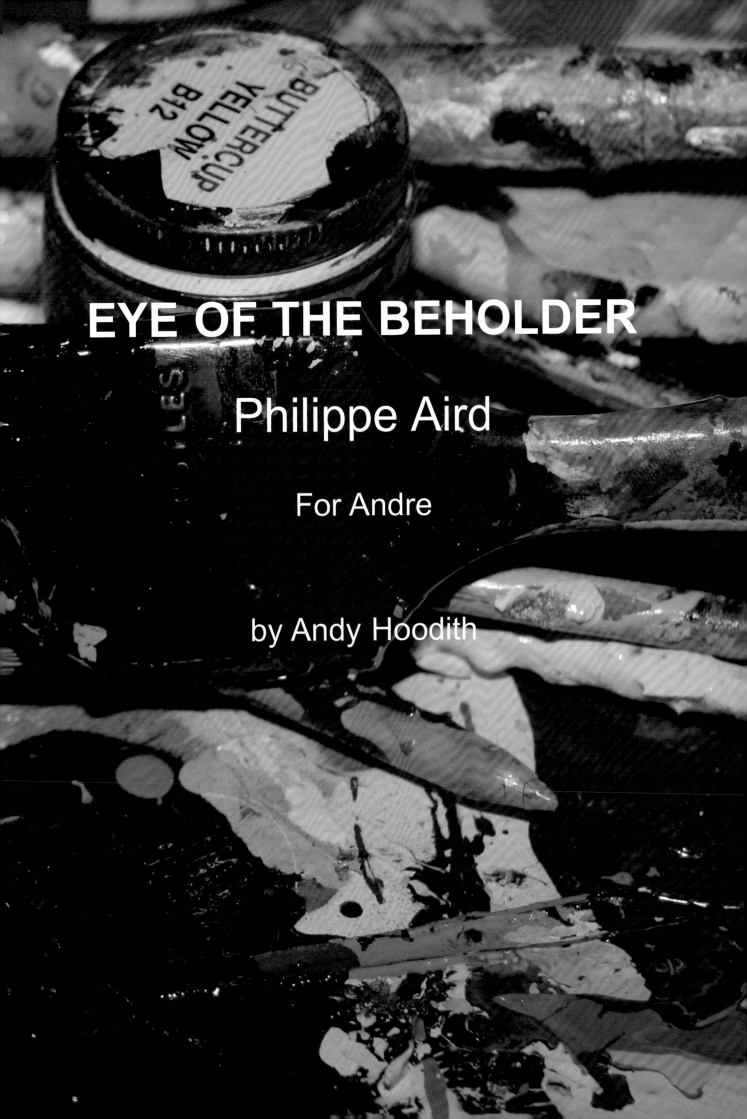

EYE OF THE BEHOLDER

Philippe Aird

For Andre

by Andy Hoodith

ACKNOWLEDGMENTS:

Design/Layout: James Bloomfield
Editing /Proof Reading: Claire Lynas
Production: Mike Lynch (MMS Media)
Photographer: Colin O'Brien
Additional Photography: Andy Hoodith, Carla Rademan

Front Cover: Gladiolus 2006
760mm x 760mm Private collection

ISBN 10 digit: 0-9554089-1-1
ISBN 13 digit: 978-0-9554089-1-5

First Edition

CONTENTS

PREFACE

Philippe Aird was first known to me as a young boy when he came to a 'Saturday Clan' I organised for children in the Natural History Museum at Buile Hill Park, Salford. He showed outstanding talent at that time, being a boy with sensitivity and gentleness in his drawing and painting.

In recent years, after his period of teaching at various colleges, he has been working on abstract images in his studio adjacent to his father's framing works in Manchester. I occasionally see flashes of colour through the doors and windows.

He has always seemed both dedicated and motivated by his work and I know this book will delight all who see it.

Harold Riley July 2006

1. Philippe Aird 1974

6

INTRODUCTION

'I hate people coming into Phoenix when I've just painted the floor...'

If you're reading this anytime between 5 am. and 4 pm. UK time, Philippe Aird is working. If you're reading it at any other time, he's probably thinking about work - or (depending on your point of view) daydreaming. In most occupations this would be a huge burden and an unhealthy state of affairs, but it seems to go with the territory of being a full-time artist - at least the territory Phil has staked out and chosen to inhabit. Consequently it is the norm for him, but Phil considers 'normal' to be a strange place to be anyway. The fact that he produces extraordinary paintings is, as this book will demonstrate, simply a by-product of his personality. Oh yes, and technique, talent, insight, empathy and a myriad of other skills and characteristics which somehow combine to produce his work. To him though, it's just a job.
Because this is a book about art, it is also a book about everything else. But let's not get bogged down in all that, for now anyway.

The morning of Saturday, March 25th 2006 has some small significance in terms of this project. It was the day Phil continued to explore techniques with his usual verve and curiosity, working outside Phoenix Gallery, where the breeze provided much-needed ventilation and space in which to avoid the paint fumes and stacks of recently-completed work. The vivid floral designs even attracted some bees and Phil had been assured by the postman that the weather would be fine. It was also the day this book was started.
After visiting an exhibition of John Thompson's in Manchester, and the launch of his book "Do You Like 'Em Then?", I realized that it was about time Phil's work was represented in a similar form. After running the idea past him we started work that afternoon. Full of enthusiasm as always, he embraced the project and the steamroller started.
I suppose we should address the questions, "why a book?' and "why now?" Well, why not? Though not really an answer, we hope that the images you see will provide sufficient reason.
Working titles included 'Nothing Personal', 'Phil Aird This Morning', 'This is Not a Book About Art' and 'Fuel for Thought'.

How did Phil select the paintings for this book? Well, the task was made easier by the fact that 90 of his paintings were stolen in 2003 (you know who you are...), but it still wasn't easy. Another hundred pieces were destroyed in a fire in a studio in Cheadle, Manchester, in the late 1990s. Luckily, Philippe Aird is prolific in the true sense - he really does paint a lot!! Even so, with numerous pieces hanging in places far and wide on at least three continents, representing Phil's artistic output from the age of 14 or earlier was no easy task. By necessity therefore, this book is a series of snapshots of the work as a whole.

The main reason that it is best to try to present Phil's work in as straightforward terms as possible is that he is a very straightforward man. He's a 'DIY' artist who would much rather make a frame than buy one, show a young painter what to do rather than tell them, and continue to build a body of work rather than bask in the comfort of his previous (considerable) achievements.

Having said that, it is natural to attempt to find a common thread or theme pervading Phil's artistic career to date. Changes in artistic style or methodology are often associated with memorable, or at least significant, events in the artist's life, such as experiences of love, death, war or illness. The personal demons which visit us all are often able to find their outlet via the creative process, and so artists are both doomed and blessed as some of the most natural communicators of our highs and lows.

Although not immediately apparent in all his work, the theme of destruction and subsequent rebirth does not just manifest itself in the name of Phil's studio/gallery. This particular Phoenix is simply the latest one to have risen out of the ashes of Phil's previous artistic incarnations. As we shall see, the courage to destroy what one has created, learn from the process and then forge relentlessly ahead is probably the most crucial characteristic in Phil's considerable armoury. At an early age he chose not to heed the advice of a world famous artist, shrugged off a lack of formal educational qualifications, embraced new media and then shunned the trappings and most of the temptations of financial success, survived the theft of many of his paintings, and, most importantly, the early death of one of his brothers, André, to whom this book is dedicated.

Amid such carnage, he has continued to develop his work, innovate and paint at a staggeringly prolific rate using all means at his disposal.

Artists - including musicians it should be said - change lives and viewpoints far more fundamentally than politicians, economists or so-called 'men of God'. This is because, as the supreme educators, they penetrate more deeply and thus get closer to who we really are. The work they produce, if we're lucky, comes from an even deeper well of consciousness and so is able to touch us directly - without words.

So, enjoy this book - and if you find something here which speaks to you, you then have the certain knowledge that you are not alone.

2. Phil and André 1963

3. Phil, André and Candy 1965

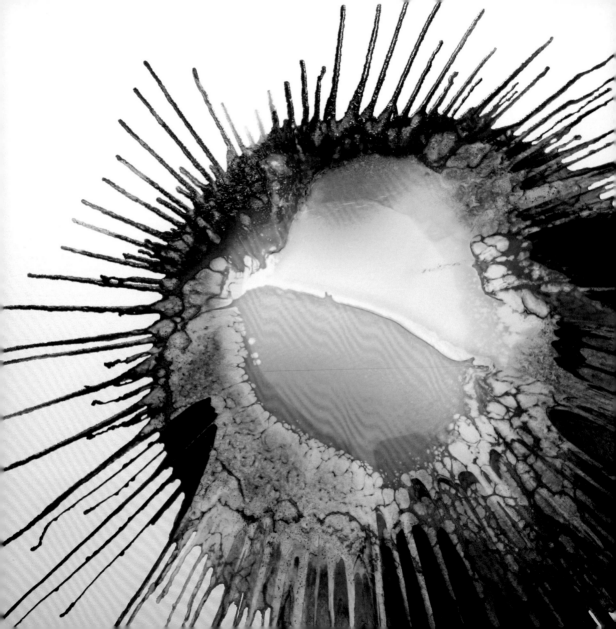

1 FORMATIVE YEARS

"I take being called a know-nothing as a compliment."

Phil's magical combinations of colour, shape and texture which adorn the walls of many living rooms, kitchens, bedrooms and offices are a world away from the pastel sky and seascapes he produced - some would say precociously - while at Cheadle Heath Primary School.

Phil's dad George, a close friend and colleague of the renowned industrial landscape artist LS Lowry, used to bring his friend's work home, and soon afterwards the man himself became a regular visitor to the Aird family home in Stockport, dropping in for Sunday lunch and a chat. He discouraged Phil from becoming an artist, labelling it 'a daft job', but this probably only encouraged the lad and made him more determined. This early trait of doggedness, combined with a willingness to take the advice of more seasoned artists with a pinch of salt, remains one of his strongest assets - if he perceives something to be a mere trend, then he'll probably buck it.

George Aird also used to take him to Buile Hill Park in Salford, where there was a mining museum. Here, another local artist, Harold Riley, held classes for the local kids, showing them the fundamentals of drawing, and Phil was one of his keenest students. In the evenings he'd be at the home of yet another artistic acquaintance of his dad's, Albin Trowsky, for more education. Phil was intrigued by Albin's wartime experiences and love of pigeons (two passions which have survived the years and are evident in Phil's everyday life), as well as his artistic techniques.

As a consequence of these close encounters with artists in action, the young lad grew rapidly in terms of real-world experience and had a far wider education than many of his more conventionally-educated peers.

George Aird comments, *'Phil has always been independent, and even I am sometimes surprised when I see his work'.*

4. L.S. Lowry, George Aird and Philippe Aird in 1970 at the Henry Donn Gallery

5. Testosterone
mixed technique on canvas 2006
930mm x 930mm.
Private Collection

Phil's mother, who he describes as the 'unsung heroine' must have been concerned at that stage that, talented though he undoubtedly was, Phil's indifference to everything except painting could seriously backfire in the future. By allowing him to find his own path from such an early age, she arguably did more than anyone to ensure that his combination of skill and enthusiasm came to fruition. Typically modest, she has remained largely in the background, but her influence has clearly been very significant. As Phil puts it, '…she's so modest but she's always been there; especially in the bad times.'

6. PIGS No.3
Mixed technique on canvas 1978
1800mm x 1200mm.
Private Collection

7. PIGS No.2
Mixed technique on canvas 1978
1800mm x 1200mm.
Private Collection

14

8. Philippe's studio at Salford University 1978

9. Life Study
Pencil on paper 1978
Private Collection

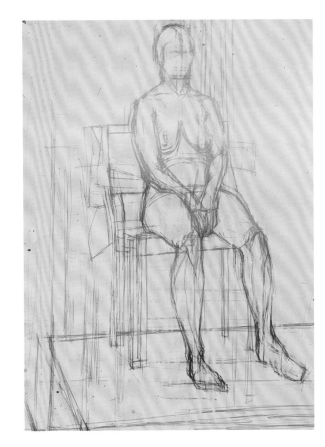

10. PIGS No.4
Mixed technique on canvas 1978
1800mm x 1200mm.
Private Collection

11. Life Study Two Figures
Pencil on paper 1978
Private Collection

16

The artistic workload taken on by Phil at this early stage would have been enough for many mature artists, and so it's not surprising (in fact it was probably inevitable) that his conventional education suffered. For a kid with a mind full of swirling shape, colour, texture and light, high school maths and geography must have seemed excruciatingly dull. But in essence the choice had already been made, driven by talent, passion and growing inner confidence.

In 1976 a London-based art dealer named George Naseby bought 28 of Phil's paintings for the equivalent of £3,000. Only a couple of years earlier he'd been too embarrassed to show his mum and dad which picture was his in an exhibition for school-children's paintings at Stockport Art Gallery. At 14, the sale of so many paintings, especially to someone in the business, so to speak, wasn't a bad start, and it gave Phil some concrete and independent proof of his talent.

Word began to spread, and at school a couple of teachers offered to buy paintings from him. He declined to sell them. His O-level art exam (taken at 16 and since replaced by the GCSE as the school-leaving exam) featured a self-portrait, with Phil on a bench in the graveyard of Cheadle Church - his own details carved into a nearby gravestone. This is heavy stuff for a teenager with his life ahead of him and it gives an early indication of his sense of mortality. Not so surprising then that the certificates of authenticity which he now gives to people who buy his paintings (since the robbery at Phoenix) are referred to - only half-jokingly - as, "Death certificates. In case I get famous!".

12. Ivan Aird, L.S. Lowry and Philippe's mother outside the family home

17

DIARY
This Morning with Philippe Aird

Phillipe Aird starts work early. By five in the morning he's at his studio-gallery near central Manchester, rummaging around for materials and methodically preparing to engage with his day's work. His main company at this time are the pigeons who have taken to cluttering about outside the back door, expectantly waiting for the daily conversation with their soul-mate - and some breakfast.

The peacefulness at this time, even within shouting distance of the hubbub to come, is extraordinary, and the mini-ecosystem in which Phil works is at its most serene. Magpies and semi-conscious revellers from the previous night share the same air, as the tarmac and flagstones prepare themselves for the daily onslaught of humanity and its debris.

Phil likes this time of day - there are very few distractions and he can simply be left to get on with his job. Phones, emails, faxes - indeed most of the things we rely on to communicate these days - are either turned off or ignored. Not the greatest fan of technology, he is consumed by the necessity of painting.

By around 11am, the bulk of the day's painting has been done and he can often be found chatting to visitors, answering correspondence, making frames, stretching canvases or looking

13. Phoenix Gallery work room 2005

18

for new avenues through which to display his work. The atmosphere is relaxed; Phil takes first-time visitors at face value, and his friendliness borders on a character defect. He often gives paintings away or sells them at what can only be described as bargain prices to people he likes.

He goes next door intermittently to see his dad at Grove Galleries. George Aird has been working for well over 50 years and is one of an ever-dwindling number of craftsmen who can restore paintings to their former glories using both the original techniques and ones he has developed himself. Phil and his dad share the all-too-rare unspoken understanding of fathers, sons and fellow artists. In short, their relationship is unique, and together with Phil's brother Ivan they represent a formidable trio, whose depth of knowledge and understanding of the practicalities and nuances of artistic techniques is difficult to match.

His working day usually finishes sometime between five and six o'clock, and to the extent that Phil has a 'typical day', that was it. Sounds great, doesn't it? However, the reality of such a life, six and a half days a week for at least fifty-one weeks of the year, including Xmas Day, is not all it might seem to be. For one thing, the sheer number of hours is staggering. Secondly, there is the constant need to create and sustain a working structure, as well as the obvious problem of motivation. This is no holiday - it's supposed to be a living, and while Phil is his own boss, a position often envied, he also the sole employee. Strip away the romanticism and there is little left except for hard work, talent, intellect and the instinct for survival. Mind you, that's a fairly useful set of attributes.

14. Detail from Figurative Painting 1983

window that his students were still sat around him on the floor engaged in animated discussion of the day's work."

This episode clearly shows where Phil's priorities lay. The art is the thing. All else comes a distant second. In this context it is hardly surprising that when he was offered a full-time and well sought-after position he showed indifference rather than joy. Of course this was much to the dismay and chagrin of the Head of Department, but an attitude which Charlie Shiels found entirely in character. As course manager, he would have dearly loved to have Phil as a permanent member of staff, but the stark truth was that the College needed him more than he needed it, and as changes took place throughout higher education in the UK, a parting of the ways was inevitable.

"This was not an environment that an artist of Phil's integrity could believe in, and he therefore made what some would see as the rash and foolhardy decision to quit completely and devote himself once again to the somewhat precarious position of being self-employed artist. However, Phil himself would probably not have seen it as a major decision, but rather a situation in which he had almost no realistic choice to make."

Charlie goes on to say that, looking back, Phil was "the complete opposite of a career teacher". In a broad sense, perhaps the best teachers usually are.
Phil's former students are now scattered far and wide, but he is still happy to give them help and advice in any way he can.

Perhaps another reason that Phil decided to stop teaching is that he realized that he was still a student in some ways. He was (and still is) constantly learning, but he is learning through autonomy, which is an inherent aspect of any journey of self-discovery. He is learning the art of fulfiling his potential, and his current studies are the epitome of 'on-the-job training' - learning by doing. The respect shown to him by students was directly proportional to their intrinsic desire to be artists, and Phil can usually spot a time-waster a mile away. That's why he was brutally honest with students who didn't seem interested. He gave them the only advice possible, considering his uncompromising approach to art; 'do something else!' On the other hand, those who chose to listen were given his time, energy, enthusiasm and glimpses into his expertise. It was then up to them to understand and use it in their own work.

16. Untitled Oil on canvas
Deloittes Collection 1983

17. Untitled Oil on canvas
Deloittes Collection 1983

18. Philippe with students from
Stockport College of Art 1982

DIARY: An Afternoon at Phoenix

The people who buy Phil's work are as many and varied as those who wander into Phoenix to browse or while away half an hour waiting to meet the estate agent and view one of the hundreds of apartments being built in this former industrial neighbourhood. Visiting the hub of Phil's activity, Phoenix Studio, which is located close to Manchester city centre, can sometimes feel like entering another world. In addition to the paintings and Phil's quirky welcome, its visitors are as disparate as the shades of light bouncing off the walls. Sitting for an afternoon at Phoenix is like being at a train station - but one minute it's on a sleepy branch line in the Lake District and the next it's Platform 3 Euston.

John, a friend and regular visitor to Phoenix, remembers being overwhelmed by the sheer variety and in your face impact of Phil's work:

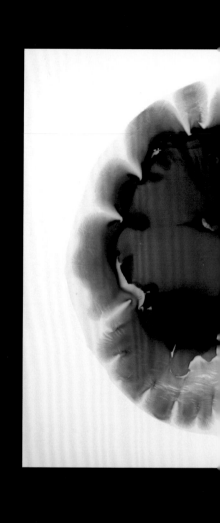

'The paintings are striking enough, but the care and craftsmanship that goes into their creation impressed me as much as the images themselves. As a glazier, I appreciate the difficulty in much of what Phil has attempted. There's simply no quick, short-cut method of producing such original artwork, and Phil and I have discussed the intricacies of glass thickness, durability, size, strength and practicality for many an hour. This type of discussion never bores him, and he soaks up the information like a sponge'.

This is a crucial aspect of Phil's accessibility, in terms of both his work and his attitude to it, and for such a shy and sometimes reclusive man, Phil is surprisingly gregarious when he feels at ease.

The fact that he is able (and usually willing) to engage in conversation about virtually anything with anyone fortunate enough to drop in is partly due to the fact that by 10 am or so, when most galleries are opening, Phil has taken care of the sharp end of painting - the painting itself - and is ready to relax and engage with the world at large. Well, almost.

In an ideal world, of course, the paintings, once dry, would then magically transport themselves to galleries, homes and offices by osmosis - preferably in exchange for reasonably large amounts of money - and Phil would be free to continue painting. It just doesn't work like that though, and so Phil, as do most artists at some point, is forced to engage in the minutiae of the art market as well as the art itself. This can involve anything from negotiating an agreement to loan his work to a company to advising a private collector on how and where to hang a particular painting. This takes considerable time and energy, as well as the patience necessary to deal with a (naturally) indecisive public. Take the following conversation:

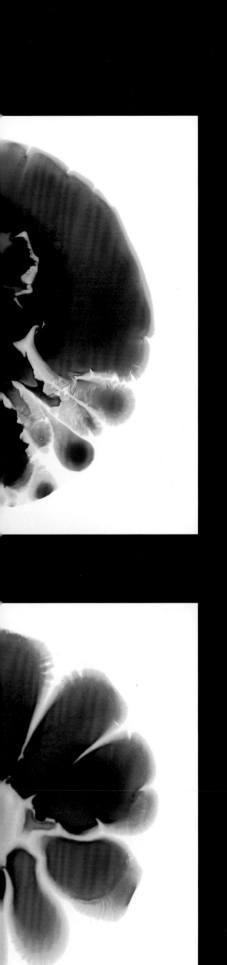

'Do you think the bluey one would look better, or the greeny flowery one?'
'Well, it depends on...'
'You know what though, I quite like the round glass one, don't you?'
'What - for the living room?'
'No, the hall',
'But it's too wide...'

This vignette is typical of dialogues at Phoenix and it illustrates a fundamental question concerning Phil's work. Is he an artist or a design consultant, and where does the line between the two become blurred? His answer would be the former (of course), but he acknowledges that in order to interact directly with clients at Phoenix he is often drawn into discussions concerning which of his paintings they should buy, where they should be displayed and even what lighting could be used to show them off to best effect in a particular room - a room in which Phil has obviously never set foot. Though he cares about such matters, he'd rather be painting.

The marketing and sale of art is a world which is difficult to fathom, especially for a newcomer. After all, what is the monetary 'value' of a painting? The short answer seems to be 'however much someone is prepared to pay for it'. But the possibility of a painting increasing in value - possibly manifold - puts an unpredictable twist in the tail of a potential sale. A cleverly-worded hint that the work has future investment potential may make the difference between someone buying or not buying.

Phil will sell his paintings to almost anyone. But the customers he most identifies with are those he has met, talked to and made some kind of human connection with, often unrelated to the painting itself. This is why he is visibly disappointed when someone in whom he has placed trust lets him down. This has happened on occasions too numerous to catalogue here.

19. Worlds Apart, Mixed technique on
    Canvas 2006 930mm x 930mm

20. Ozone Mixed technique on
    Canvas 2006 930mm x 930mm

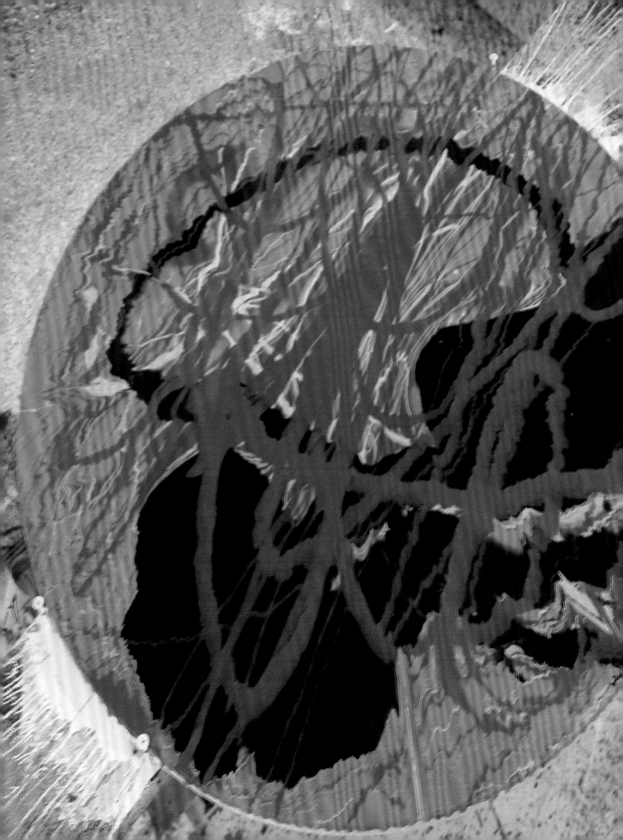

3 A LEAP OF FAITH: GOING IT ALONE

To commit oneself to the challenge of earning a living by painting is a step into the unknown, and the attrition rate is high. The very fact that Phil is still at work is unusual; the reality often bites hard for those who make the leap, and many revert to the safety of a 'regular' income. But it's worth noting that for every artist who has tried, a thousand or more wish they had. It probably isn't primarily to do with money though, it's more likely related to the fact that if they don't bite the bullet and make that leap they'll never know if they could have made a go of it. In this sense, such regrets are not so different from any other musings on unfulfilled potential, be they artistic, literary, sporting or political.

Before working at Vernon and Albert Mills, and prior to opening Phoenix, Phil produced a large body of work at home. Unfortunately, little of this remains, as he has the somewhat rash habit of destroying chunks of work - either dumping them in the nearest skip for some lucky 'collector' to find, or otherwise disposing of them.

One of the paintings he produced at his home on Reservoir Street was loosely entitled '*(Zinadine) Zidane and the Salford Slappers*'. For many, the title alone would indeed be a puzzle - encased in a mystery and wrapped in an enigma. But if you know a bit about football and are from the north of England then it at least begins to make some sort of sense.

However, it's worth mentioning that he says, looking back a mere five years or so, that, '*Living among my paintings seems a bit daft now. It's a puzzle*'.

He currently works among his paintings - a crucial difference, though on the surface only a geographical one. But if we liken this to someone working from home as opposed to an office, the effect becomes more understandable. In typical contrary style then, while many people in so-called developed societies yearn to move from the workplace to the home, Phil's trend has been in the opposite direction!

Since moving to Ellesmere Street, Manchester, from Stockport in 2003, Phil has been broadening his range of work. The move came about as a result of the Cheshire Fire Brigade's insistence that the artistic activities at Vernon Mill in Stockport be terminated for safety reasons.

Phil's fascination with the physical relationships among materials, be they paint, glass, wood, metal or plastic, is clearly

21. Molten Furnace, Mixed technique on glass 2006 1000mm diameter

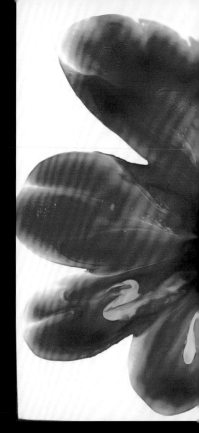

evident in each piece he produces. Working at Vernon Mill in the early 90s, the industrial theme is present, if not overtly in the subject matter, then certainly in the methodology; the furnace and white heat melding the raw materials and transporting us back to the smelting pots of the age of mass industrialization. The viewer is reminded of steeplejack and industrial enthusiast Fred Dibner or a fevered medieval figure bent over a crucible, as much as Jackson Pollock or Francis Bacon.

This obsession with breaking new ground in his art can be compared with the ancient search for the formula which would have allowed the alchemists to produce gold. Simply put, rather than seeking the pot at the end of the rainbow - clearly an absurd ambition - the alchemists sought to make the stuff themselves. Phil's approach is similarly practical; he takes the spectrum of the rainbow itself and creates something new. Rather than theorize or fantasize about the nuts and bolts of the cosmos, he tries to recreate them on canvas. Well, if you're going to recreate, why settle for bits of the jigsaw, why not go for the whole cosmos?

However, it is important to remember here that his search is not primarily motivated by the end product itself. The fascination is in the process, rather than the product - curiosity is the key. While other artists may settle on a technique they have mastered, Phil's restlessness drives him to the next step.

22. Narcissus
    Mixed Technique on Canvas 2006
    930mm x 930mm

23. Cosmos
    Mixed Technique on Canvas 2006
    930mm x 930mm

24. Zinnia
    Mixed Technique on Canvas 2006
    930mm x 930mm

His work during this period signifies another staging post on the road to the present and gives us several hints as to his potential. But to second-guess and predict what he'll do next is impossible.

During the 80s and 90s Phil's work came to the attention of the general public in a variety of ways, not least the BBC documentary on him which aired in the spring of 1992. With growing interest from buyers, exhibitions in Edinburgh and Los Angeles, and a steady supply of compliments, Philippe Aird was, to all intents and purposes, on the fast track to 'success'. However, the maxim, 'Be careful what you ask for, you might get it', springs to mind here, because Phil found that the destination wasn't nearly as interesting and rewarding as the journey. His time and commitment were in demand from all quarters and the mental space he needed to work was being crowded out by other concerns. The money, while welcome at first, eventually became part of the problem, and he withdrew from the limelight so that he could restore some semblance of order to his work and his life. To achieve this he somewhat surprisingly decided to return to basics and produced only still life paintings for over a year. The contrast between this and the cutting-edge work which had proved so 'successful' could hardly have been greater. But by going back to the fundamentals of his craft, Phil found a new sense of direction and managed to avoid the traps and trappings of what can loosely be described as the celebrity art world.

The mill in which Phil currently works was established as the home of George Aird's Grove Galleries in May, 2003. By this time, Phil was very well versed in the intricacies of restoration, a dying art which his father and a handful of others have kept alive amid the mad scramble for the new. Ask any painter, frame-maker or serious artist around the north-west of England if they've heard of Grove and you'll probably get a knowing 'yes'. Previously based at Albert Mill - which itself is currently being absorbed into the new urbanized, residential centrifuge - Grove effectively served as one of the main locations for Phil's continuing apprenticeship. This may sound strange given his age and experience, but it reflects his continuing growth and the enduring nature of his curiosity. The regular flow of artists - including Harold Riley and Geoffrey Key - who visit his dad, whether for advice, technical know-how or simply a chat, have provided an invaluable human resource for Phil. He in turn has shown respect and admiration for their skills, and rather than eschewing the traditions of his craft, he has embraced them wholeheartedly.

Phil's restoration work highlighted the blending of the traditional and modern which occur on a daily basis between Grove and Phoenix.

"With restoration work", Phil says, *"every piece is absolutely unique, needing different potions in order to restore their former glory. It takes total concentration, sometimes working for weeks on one painting, and in this sense it's a complete contrast to my own work.*

The techniques themselves include removing the effects of smoke, nicotine, decorating materials and remedying an assortment of mishaps. Like the Renaissance Madonna and Child which some careless builder had managed to impale on a plank.

25. Phoenix Gallery 2004

26. George Aird at Grove Galleries 2006

27. Philippe Restoring at Grove Galleries 2002

28. Tree Paintings

30

Paintings have to be restored using a wide range of materials, from rabbit skin glue to beeswax, and the fusing and cleaning using medical swabs is akin to surgery – even down to the plastic gloves, boxes of which can be found in both Grove and Phoenix.

The broadening of Phil's experience at the Vernon and Albert Mills, and the freedom he enjoyed to develop his own work, is continually apparent in his work. The carpentry and furniture-making skills, the inner workings of framing machinery and the varying strengths and weaknesses of canvases are all understood at a deep level, thus enabling him to be more or less self-sufficient (i.e. not reliant on others to complete any given task in the production of his work). One gets the feeling that if he had time he'd build a greenhouse from scratch and produce his own food.

But time can only be pursued, not captured, though this seems to be one of the main driving forces behind his work - the attempt to blend a moment in time with the flow of time itself. If astrophysics terminology were to be applied, it would be something akin to a 'unifying theory' of abstract art - except that its application is concrete rather than theoretical.

DIARY: Dropping in

A recent visitor to Phoenix, swanning around the studio with the largely misguided confidence that comes with years of value judgments, told Phil the order in which a couple of paintings had been completed. In fact, this critic was so perceptive that he even told Phil which one was 'better'! Despite the fact that he was wrong about the chronology and unaware of the absurdity of his second pronouncement, Phil was bemused rather than annoyed by this ridiculous attempt to provide a five minute critique of his latest work.

Phil's artistic output doesn't need the validation of those who set themselves up as part-time experts. Separating the wheat from the chaff in page after page of jargonistic meandering merely alienates most ordinary people, and so the aim of making modern art more accessible can, especially at the pen of those with a premeditated critical agenda, become lost in the fog of fancy-dan indulgence. Simply stated, you don't really need to explain why you like a painting - you just do. So we're back to the emotional response versus the critical one: gut instinct versus a more objective but ultimately less satisfying analysis.

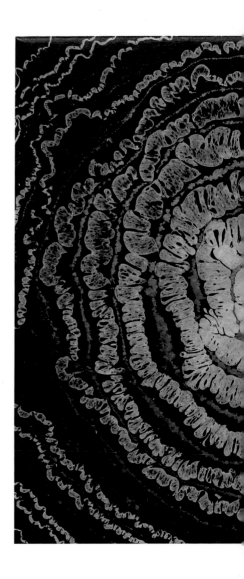

The need to verbalise and narrate a painting is another expression of our inability to simply accept it for what it is and how it makes us feel. However, it is also an entirely understandable reaction because when we see something about which we feel strongly, then it's natural for us to want to communicate that to others. We can't always show the other person the image that has stimulated us and so we settle for second or third best - a lexical description, either via conversation or the written word. Even though we know our attempts to transpose the emotion are doomed to failure, we attempt it anyway. This is OK up to a point, but if we

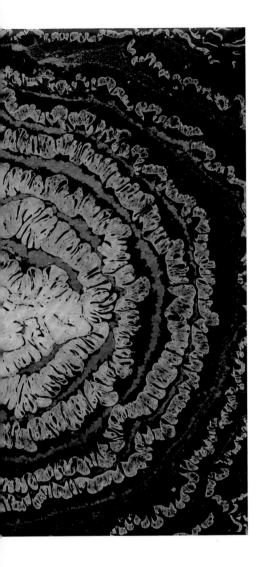

take one or more of Phil's paintings and presume to draw broad general truths - or even theories - about the motivations and 'hidden' meanings therein, we run the risk of alienating all but those who share that particular way of reacting to art. On the one hand, this does the art and the artist a great disservice, but on the other it sometimes results in the work being taken more 'seriously' in the more rarified world of art criticism.

In any case, the view of one critic is highly unlikely to cause Phil any lost sleep. He seems to listen as intently to the views of the postman as to anyone else. To some extent he draws inspiration from the comments and observations of almost everyone who drops by - as long as they haven't shown early signs of being too 'up themselves'. He is also aware that art galleries can tend to make people feel slightly uncomfortable at times - many don't know how to behave, as though there was some kind of code of conduct for looking at paintings. There is sometimes a palpable '...is it OK if we look at the paintings?' feel from some visitors, while at the other end of the scale there are those who sprint round as though they're doing last minute Christmas shopping. Phil tries to put visitors at ease - or maybe it's that Phil himself is completely at ease within Phoenix - and so their reactions to his work are immediately supported by their interaction with him. There is no 'gap' between the art and the artist.

29. Red Vortex Paintings in Situ

30. Jazz Painting 600mm x 600mm
    Mixed technique on canvas 2004

31. Jazz Painting No.4 600mm x 600mm
    Mixed technique on canvas 2004

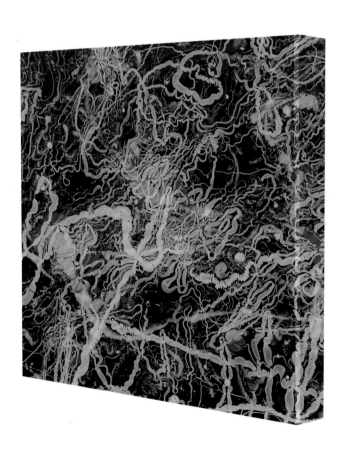

33

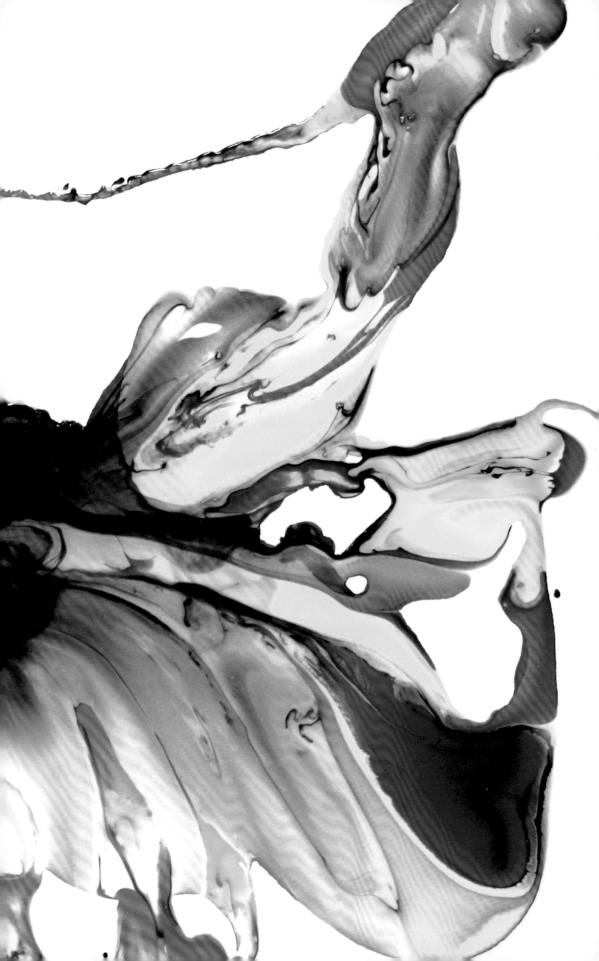

4 PHOENIX NIGHTMARE

"That one's definitely a spider"

In mid-July 2003, the day after Phil had opened Phoenix Studio to the public (to coinciding with his 42nd birthday), thieves broke in and stole ninety paintings, several of which were by other artists, including *'The Dome Café'* by Charlie Shiels. Opening Phoenix had cost a bob or two and having the place fitted with a burglar alarm wasn't considered an absolute priority at the initial stage. Neither was insurance.

Around twenty people had attended the opening, and he was 'quite pleased with it as a start'. The vast majority of the paintings were Phil's work - about five years worth of it - but he was most upset by the fact that the work of others had been stolen. As he told the Manchester Evening News:

'I'd wanted to open my own gallery for years. It's taken a while for this to sink in but the more I think about it the more gutting it is. The worst thing about the whole affair is that I feel guilty and partly responsible for the artists' work that I was keeping there. It's one thing to have your own work stolen but to lose someone else's is a terrible feeling'.

The photograph accompanying the article showed more than a bewildered artist looking at the absence of his own memories. It shows a man wondering whether or not it's worth all the hassle, this art thing. It seems to say, *'OK, so all property is theft - what have you stolen lately?'*

Those paintings and photographs are now in the murky world of stolen art, and although they don't have the monetary value of a couple of missing Gainsboroughs or a Gaugin or three (though Charlie's painting was valued at £5,750), their significance to Phil is without measure. The time, effort, experience and creativity spent on producing that body of work is irreplaceable. But to the thief, as to the true cynic, the price means everything and the real value means nothing.

However, this episode is not a sob story, just a way of illustrating that a painting has a value and a life independent of its price, its owner and its creator. So the missing Airds, be they in Ireland or Iowa, have made their own way in the world. Even if the thieves were stupid enough to destroy or damage the paintings, the resulting smoke and dust would simply be returning them to their origins as pigments and combinations of light and heat.

Should this image seem a little esoteric it is because the physical, cosmic and microscopic world is very apparent in Phil's current output. Three years on from the robbery, the walls at Phoenix are full again and Phil's intuition has continued to manifest itself in shape, colour and texture.

32. The Circus detail

Even so, ninety paintings is a lot, and the chances of at least a few of them surfacing in a gallery or at an auction at some point is reasonably high, as will be the price. So if anyone reading this has a clue or two it may be worth returning them, as Phil is well-known for his generosity.

Understandably, the robbery had a huge impact on Phil's attitude, particularly in its immediate aftermath. Soon after the event an art student wandered unknowingly into Phoenix and was 'interrogated,' as Phil puts it. Paranoia set in for a while, but was counterbalanced by the continuing interest in his paintings and his belief - not only in himself but in others. This was confirmed when a couple came in, bought two paintings, stayed to chat for a while and have since been annual visitors, usually purchasing at least one piece to add to their growing collection. These kinds of relationships are crucial to him maintaining what is essentially an optimistic view of the world.

In retrospect, the irony of the robbery is that Phil is now somehow grateful to the thieves for their unwitting contribution to his development. The decks had been cleared for him and the only meaningful way forward was to paint his way through the situation. Having made the decision to open Phoenix, the lack of paintings to display was a problem that could only be remedied by rolling his sleeves up and getting on with it. The alternative would have been to 'cave in' and let the disappointment and sense of injustice overwhelm him. This isn't to say that he simply shrugged off the event and continued as before. The robbery

33. Phoenix Studio 2005

34. Phoenix Studio 2005

35. Phoenix Studio 2003

36

didn't just affect his head and his heart; it inevitably made him more guarded about the casual visitors and the issue of security. But in the end, he feels that if someone - be they a stealer of paintings or ideas - is intent on ripping him off, then ultimately it's their loss.

Phil's instinctive DIY approach to his life and art presented him with many tasks to keep him busy in the rebuilding process. Putting together workbenches and installing the machinery necessary to take his 'spinning' ideas to the next stage was both time-consuming and physically tiring, as was the painting process itself. Having always wrestled with the question, 'What is work?', Phil tends towards the view that almost anything worthwhile is the result of 95% perspiration and 5% inspiration. This is entirely consistent with his insistence that he 'follows' rather than directs the way in which his work develops. The work is almost self-generating, with the artist as both fuel and engine. The dynamism of Phil's imagination provides the rest. The destination remains tantalizingly unclear until it is reached.

Whatever the process of repopulating Phoenix, the results served to confirm Phil's ability to forge ahead and produce work which sparks more than casual interest. Within a year of the robbery, he had an exhibition at the Farmilo Fiumano gallery in London, and the following year a prominent presence at the Manchester Art Show. He was also featured in 'City Life', Manchester's equivalent to London's 'Time Out', and had a steady stream of customers, both at Phoenix and from the network of people who had been following his work over the years. Several galleries were also very supportive, as were his family and close friends.

This support reflects a natural tendency among those who meet Phil to want to help him. But this does not derive out of sympathy. Rather, it is the result of spending half an hour or so with him and seeing clearly the lack of artistic pretense and the genuine interest in others that he displays. It's a two-way relationship though. Phil listens and picks up on comments people make, whether directly related to art or not. Once his daily painting is done and dusted - and if he's happy with it - he's content to engage in conversations ranging from the intricacies of drill bits to the pros and cons of euthanasia. He sees practical applications to his art in virtually everything, and this is why he simply cannot stop innovating.

DIARY: How Does He Do It?

Two ideas are virtually compulsory in answering this chapter's question; inspiration and technique.

To identify, (or even discuss) inspiration seems something of a cliché - particularly in relation to a living artist. For one thing, it assumes that he has the answer to the question 'What inspires you?' Secondly, it presupposes that inspiration can be conveniently boxed and presented in 26 symbols (plus spaces and punctuation…) so that the reader can 'understand' the artist's work more fully. Thirdly, assuming that the artist acknowledges that he cannot fully describe what inspires him, the writer has then to second-guess in order to come up with some kind of explanation. This is very difficult. In addition, it somehow misses the point of this book, which is to show a contemporary artist in full flow.

'Technique' is yet another word which is over-used, whether it be in contemporary modern art, ballet, football or golf. It is also another unavoidable issue in any serious discussion of Phil's work.

So what are Philippe Aird's techniques? You won't find the answer between these pages - at least not in black and white. Most artists probably wouldn't tell you anyway, but it's worth remembering that 'breaking the rules' is usually much more meaningful when you know what the rules are, and Phil's instinct is to do just that.

It seems that most artists have two, maybe three sustainable ideas in their lifetimes. If they can translate these onto canvas (or into their chosen medium), then they're usually content for a while. Some are so content they repeat what is essentially the same idea

36. Yu-Ka-Ri Mixed Technique on Canvas
   1750mm x 1000mm

for years, become very successful - critical acclaim can turn swiftly into monetary reward - and then… what? Have another idea? Maybe.

Phil used to tell his students at Stockport College that he should have been a dustman covering London's South Kensington during the 80s. He'd come to the conclusion that Francis Bacon couldn't possibly have produced what were to become some of his most iconic and controversial paintings without having made extensive preparatory drawings.

This turned out to be correct, as the later discovery (after Bacon's death) of many of the sketches proved. They were subsequently valued in the millions, providing an invaluable insight into the preparatory work which Bacon consistently denied, or at least played down. But the lesson Phil (and perhaps his students) took from this is that it is well nigh impossible to just produce brilliant work without the honing of technique and the courage to delve into emotional and psychological areas which many prefer to repress.

It is said that Francis Bacon walked into a gallery in London one day, wrote a cheque for a very considerable amount for one of his own paintings, took it outside and destroyed it. In the summer of 2006 a 'collector' of Phil's work was captured on CCTV clambering out of a skip with an unwanted canvas under his arm. The irony of the Bacon connection was not lost on Phil, and produced a wry smile - 'good luck to him', being his only comment. This was one of hundreds of paintings which eventually find their way in the world - starting out at Phoenix and contributing to their creator's journey.

Because Phil's work is in and of the moment - almost Zen-like in its spontaneity - it is extremely difficult to arrive at a satisfactory description of his technique. What the viewer sees is an amalgamation of techniques refined and overlaid through trial and error, time and time again.

The question remains though - how does he do it? Well, on a purely mechanical level, Phil's techniques are varied to say the least, and perhaps in the end it doesn't really matter. To deduce the techniques from the paintings themselves is part of the game that many artists, wannabes and critics play to pass the time, get a degree or 'discuss' art instead of doing it. The alchemy of the artist is as intriguing as that of the statistician - and twice as perplexing.

Visiting Phoenix is certainly an education. But if you really want to know how he does it then just ask him. He might even tell you!! For me, it's a lot to do with shape, colour, texture, gravity, chaos and intensity. And paint.

37. Philippe at the Phoenix
Studio 2006

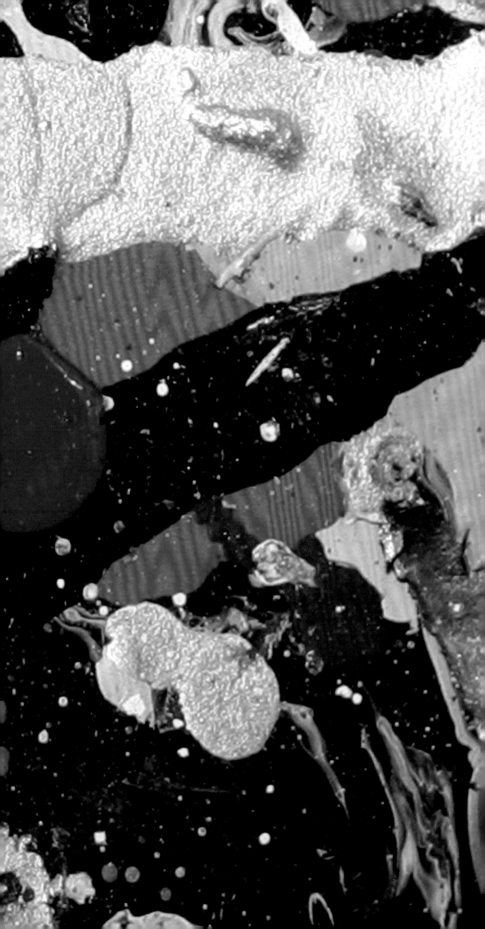

5 PHOENIX RISING

"How did you find this place then?"

In the summer of 2003, back on track and with renewed vigour, Phil set about the task of rebuilding Phoenix with characteristic gusto. His work ethic, ingrained since childhood and exemplified by his father, manifested itself again as he threw himself into his paintings and put the robbery behind him. He was shaken and also stirred.

Several months later and with the Manchester Fine Art Show fast-approaching, it was all hands on deck at Phoenix. The paintings for the show had to be selected, transported to the venue, hung properly within the parameters of the event, and then, all being well, sold! The perfectionist in Phil took over, and every aspect of his space was given care and due attention.

The preparations for the show had begun about a month or so prior to the event and continued until it opened at 10 o'clock on the preview day. Almost immediately, Phil started chatting to those with whom he feels most at home - ordinary, no frills, down-to-earth people. That's not to say he felt uncomfortable with those whose reactions were more esoteric, it was simply that his nervousness was quelled more by a good joke shared with a passer-by (which often led on to a more in-depth chat about the work), than by the more earnest attempts to analyse the work without much of a conversational prelude.

By lunchtime the GMEX Exhibition Hall wasn't exactly throbbing with visitors, although the morning had seen Phil's paintings tweak the interest of more than a few passers by:

"That one's definitely a spider'.
'Do you think so, it's more like a cherry tree I think....."

In fact, the work was causing something of a stir, not least among the other exhibitors. Much of the other work on display could easily be categorized, but Phil's paintings consistently challenged observers and caused many a double-take.

In setting up the display, the task of condensing Phil's world at Phoenix amid the chaotic hubbub of the show's preparations had been a difficult task. Phil's attitude was typically hands on, and he even found time to help others, despite his obvious nervousness. During the show itself he frequently nipped out for a breather, and while attending his own work he was clearly pleased to see a familiar face or three among the hundreds of perusers.

In terms of selling his work, things weren't going particularly well, and in truth the only thing keeping Phil and his paintings at

GMEX was the inherent optimism that pervades even the darker side of his personality. Outside, on the steps confronting the Midland Hotel, the mutterings of discontent among the art dealers; 'not as good as last year', 'the weather could have been better' (it was clear sunny day and a balmy 23°C) sounded ominous. The afternoon bought more of the same in terms of weather but a change of fortune - at least for Phil - in terms of concrete interest in his work. In just over three hours he had sold enough paintings to cover the costs of renting the space and the morning's doubts had evaporated in the Manchester sunshine.

The Sunday brought more comments on Phil's work and more people who wanted part of it in their homes. The most negative comment was *'Well, it's a bit modernistic'*, which is hardly a criticism. The interpretation of this assessment is best left to others. Perhaps the key word over which critics may argue is 'bit'. Other than that, the adjectives were resoundingly encouraging. *'A wonderful splash of colour'*, *'Very unusual and high impact artwork'*, *'The lobster looks great!'*. The poodle, trees, roots, planets, oil puddles, tears, implosions, Star Wars set-scapes, half-digested pizzas and a myriad other interpretations were also both heartfelt and apposite.

Of all the comments, both offhand and considered, the one made by 6-year-old Zak identified with a single word - *'explosion!'* - the birth of the universe as one of the themes which can be read into Phil's work. The chances of this being mere coincidence are remote. At that age, unencumbered by the baggage of previous critical input, he simply described what he saw.

The good weather lasted just about as long as the show, and with May Day literally on the horizon Phil went back to Phoenix with a wry smile on his face, no doubt fuelled by the fact that not only had people appreciated the work, but that there'd been some fierce craic in between the bouts of 'art talk'.

At the end of the show John and Colin (who as we shall see later are long-time allies of Phil's in the struggle against categorization and control), whisked the paintings back down the road amid a brief downpour and the nest of the Phoenix was restored - well, almost - to its former state. The difference was the absence of several paintings, gone to pastures new with proud owners, and the imminent departure of a lot more.

38. The Super Nova series
    mixed technique on canvas
    2005

39. Fireball No.4
    Mixed Technique on Canvas
    600mm x 600mm 2004

40. Dragonfly
   Mixed Technique on Canvas
   600mm x 900mm 2006

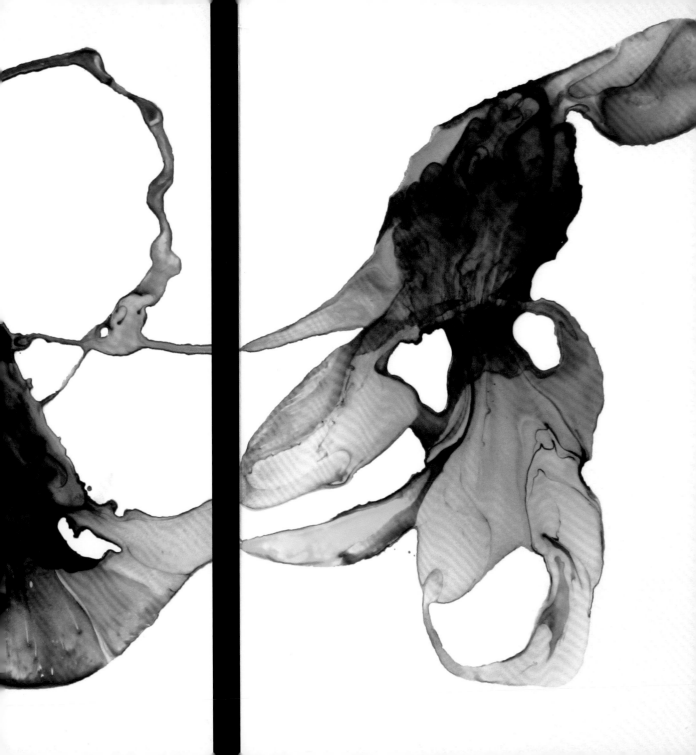

Seeing Phil's work, both old and new, for the first time in February 2006, I was struck by its chaotic nature. The Big Bang, macroscopic images and the almost bacterial detail of some of the work strongly suggested many elements related to Chaos Theory. Sensitive dependence on initial conditions - temperature, fluidity, density, mass and external - and, crucially, unpredictable - forces, combine to devastating effect in Phil's work. But they combine only once in each painting, and once the chemical reaction has taken place then the result is permanent. He governs the initial conditions as best he can, just as meteorologists (or econometrists) do everything in their power to create as perfect a starting point as possible before running simulations of the weather or the trends on Wall Street. But Phil departs from the theorists in one simple way. The end product, incontrovertible and bold, is there for all to see.

Gravity, light, the forces of nature acting on the different viscosities of the paints, happenstance, and Phil's personality are expressed in these paintings, and the fact that they communicate meaning to others is simply a happy outcome of his hard work.

Generally speaking, people wandering into Phoenix are pleasantly surprised by what they find. There are times though, when the expectations of visitors are not met, as was the case in 2005 when a website salesman unwittingly stumbled in on Phil, at work in Phoenix with his trousers down and wearing a dust mask and surgical gloves! His pants had descended due to his belt coming undone while delicately transporting a painting across the studio. Unable to pull them up without damaging the painting he was caught in a seemingly inexplicable situation and needless to say his poor visitor put two and two together, made five, and ran a mile.

In contrast, a few weeks later a couple came into the gallery, one of whom was blind. It was late afternoon and Phil was looking forward to getting home and tuning out to his favourite TV re-run, 'The World at War'. He was intrigued however, by the idea of how a blind person could relate to his paintings, and the recently completed 'Eye' suddenly held further significance. The visitor was guided to the painting and encouraged to run her hand over its surface while the image was described orally. Nearly an hour later the visitors left, but the experience has lingered and remains etched in his mind.

The idea that abstract art can communicate in ways in which figurative art cannot is not a new one. But to see this firsthand is quite powerful, as Janet Lewis, Director of Heathlands Village Residential Home can attest. She sees those suffering from dementia as constantly looking for something which is basically intangible, and the bare and often dull walls of many such homes are likely to instill little more than despair among the residents. Even figurative paintings are something of a let-down, she

41. Phoenix Studio 2005

46

42. Hawk Eye
   Mixed Technique on Canvas
   930mm 930mm 2006

thinks, because whatever it is the people are looking for, it usually isn't a particular portrait or landscape or bowl of fruit. However, an abstract image gives pause for thought simply because it isn't a painting 'of' something. It's just there. It might be a face, it might be a hat, it could just as easily be an elephant. The very vagueness of the image stimulates thought, interpretation and sometimes discussion. She is quick to point out that the image might not be what the resident is searching for, but the internal 'conversation' with the painting and any overt discussion of it, is therapeutic in itself.

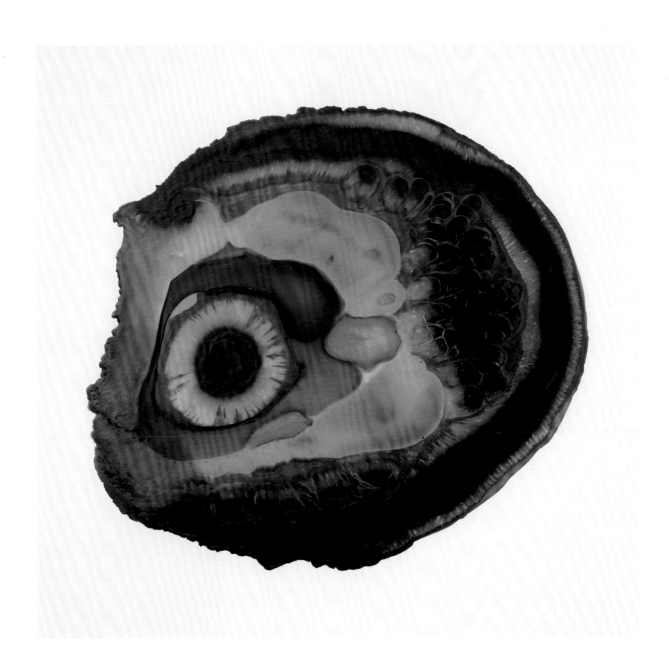

Colour Plates

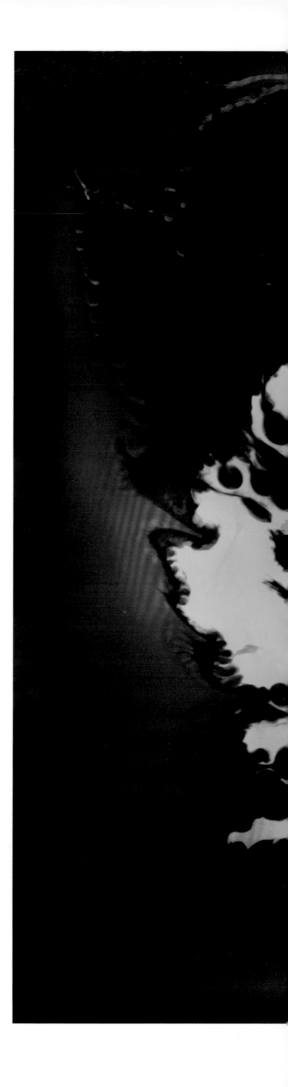

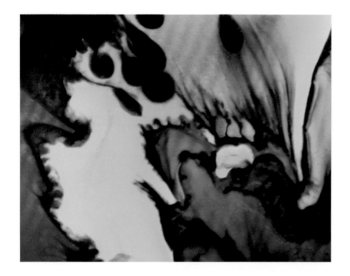

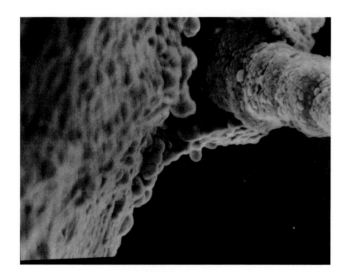

43. Gladiolus detail

44. Phil's sketchbook (archive images)

45. Gladiolus
    Mixed Technique on Canvas
    760mm 760mm 2006

Philippe

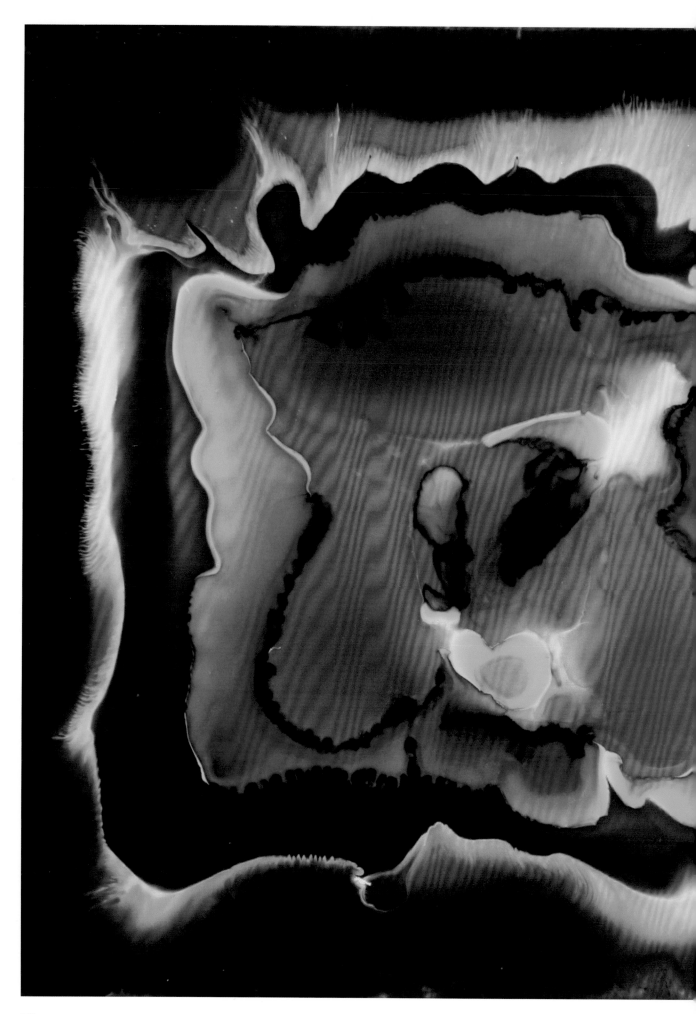

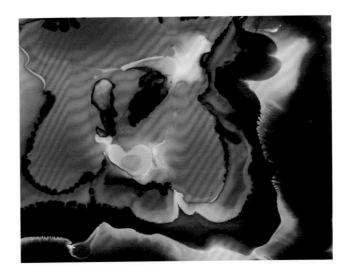

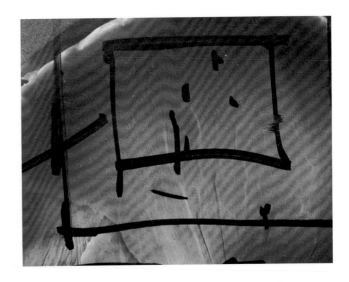

46. Phil's sketchbook (archive images)

47.Aurora
   Mixed Technique on Canvas
   760mm x 760mm 2006

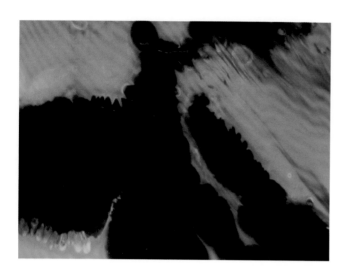

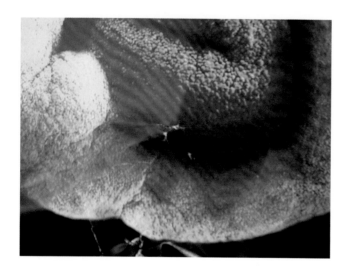

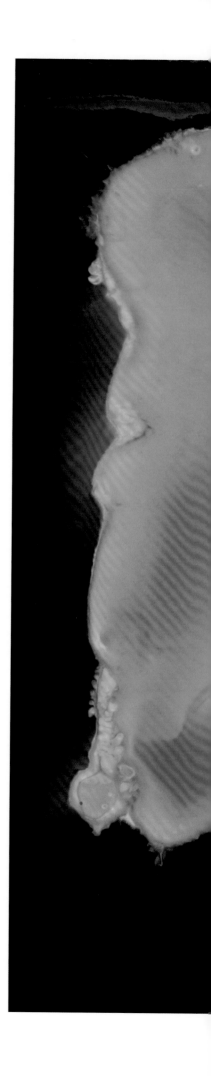

48. Detail of Vestibular system

49. Phil's sketchbook (archive image)

50. Vestibular System
   Mixed Technique on Canvas
   760mm x 760mm 2006

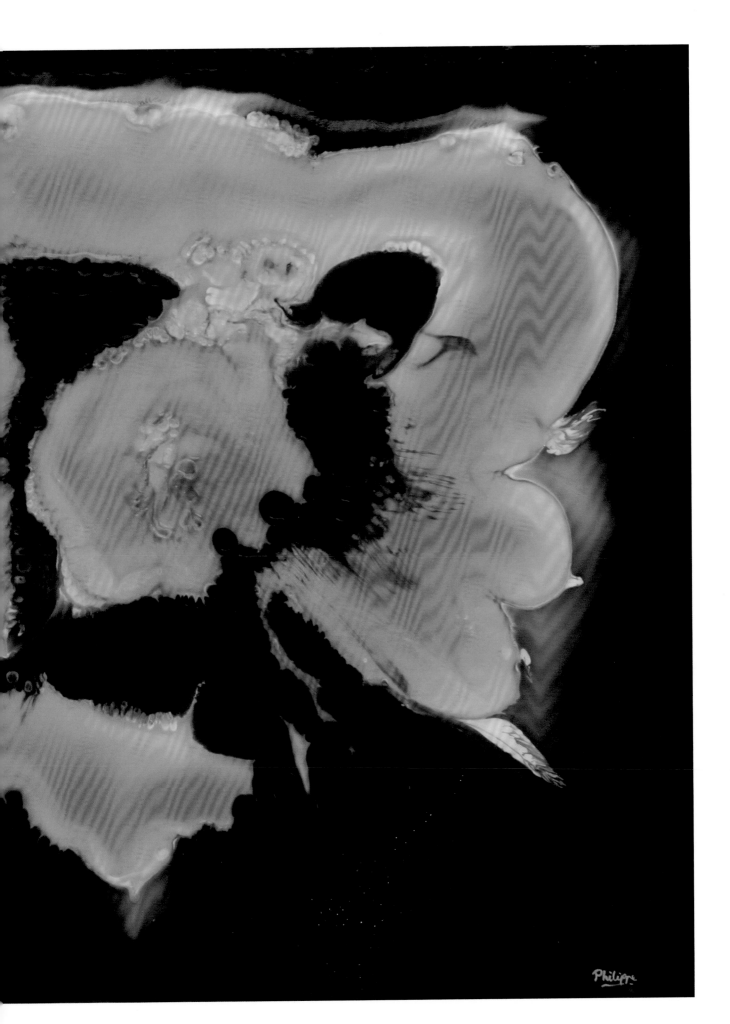

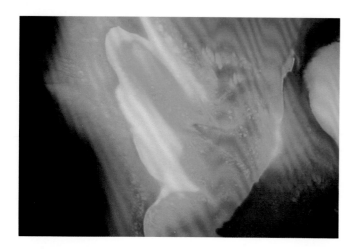

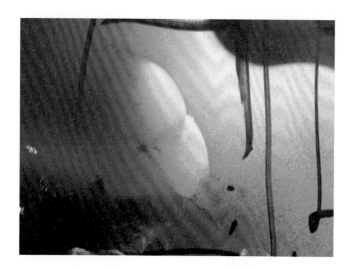

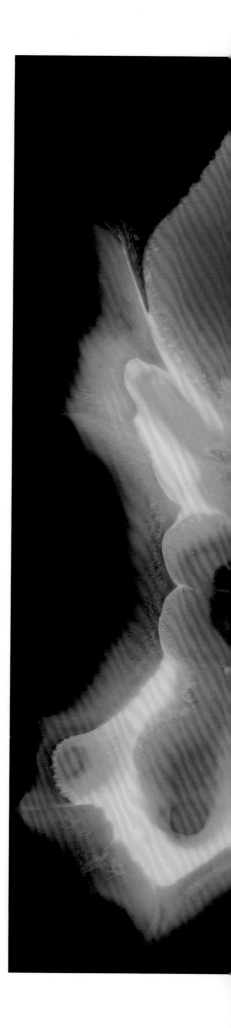

51. Melatonin detail

52. Phil's sketchbook (archive image)

53. Melatonin
Mixed Technique on Canvas
760mm x 760mm 2006

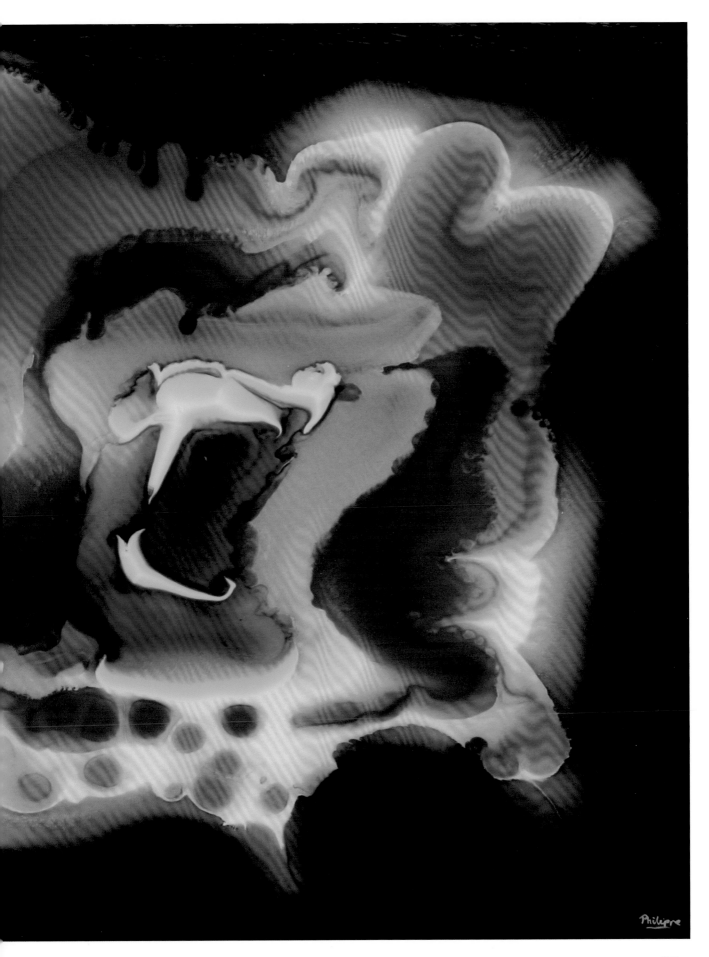

Philippe

54. Stellar
Mixed Technique on Canvas
760mm x 760mm 2006

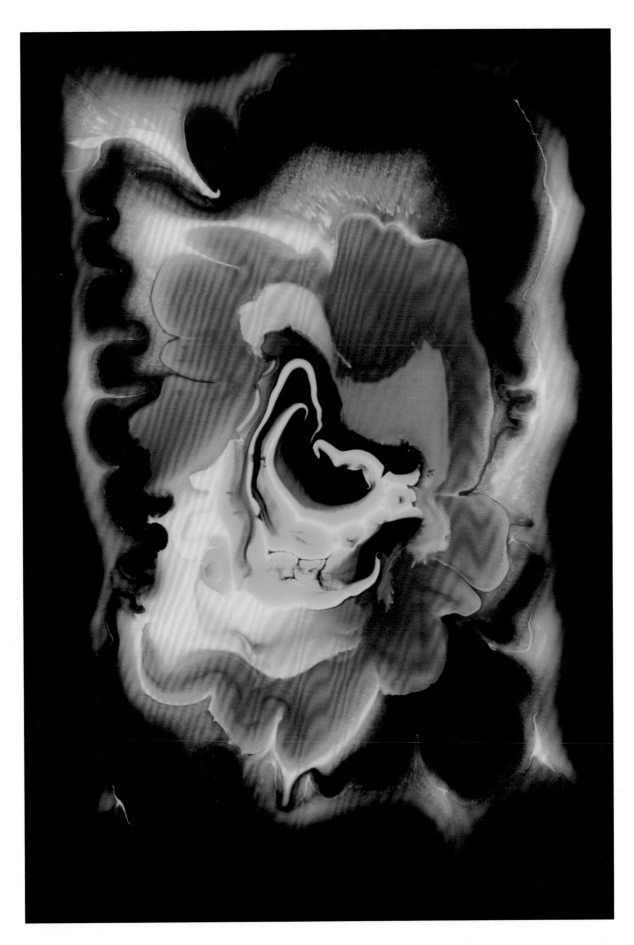

55. Magellow
Mixed Technique on Canvas
760mm x 760mm 2006

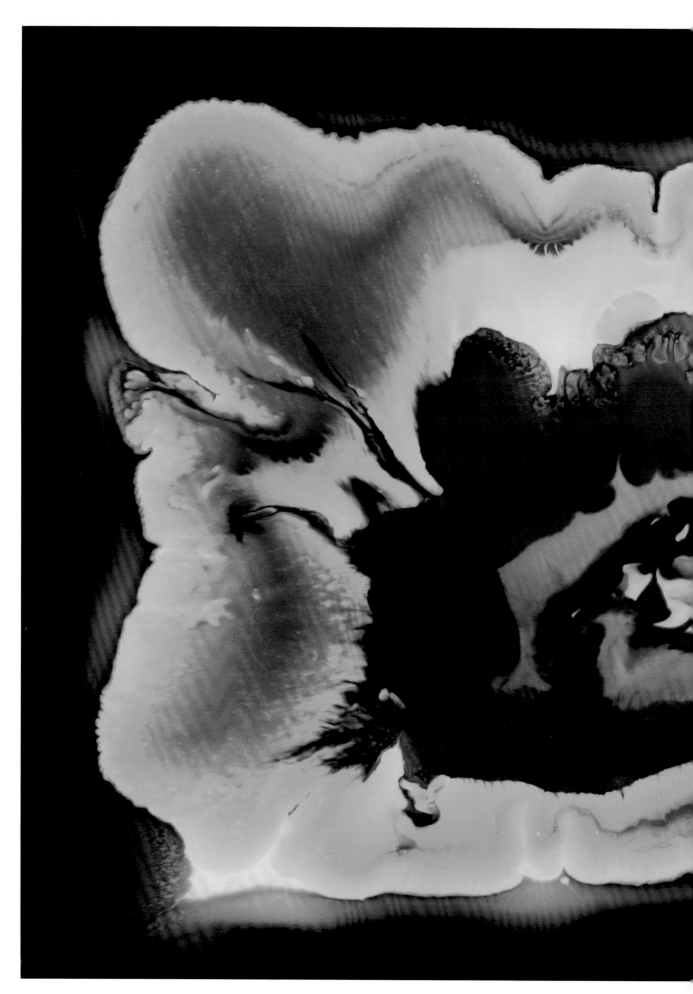

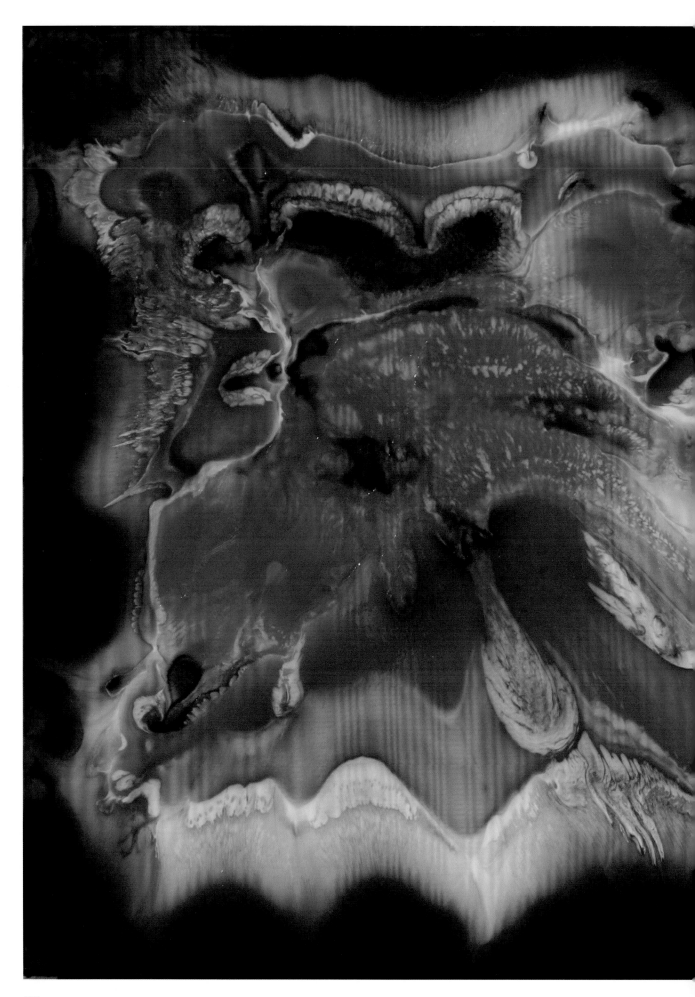

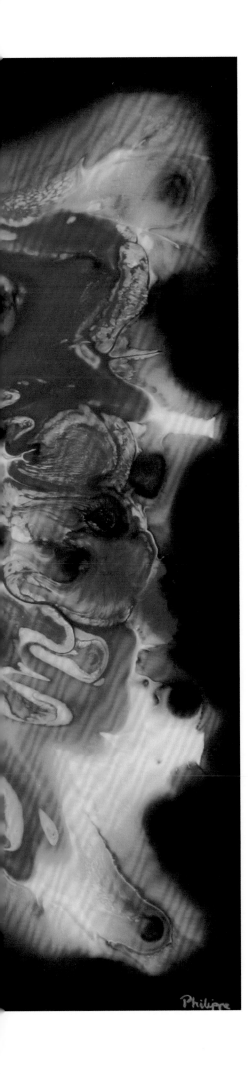

56. Hydra (previous page)
    Mixed Technique on Canvas
    760mm x 760mm 2006

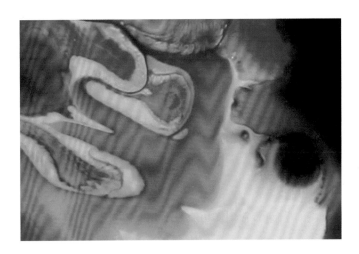

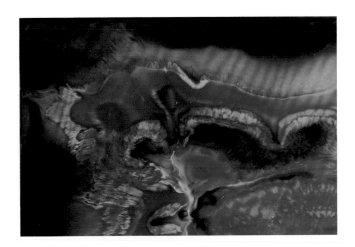

57. Dorado detail

58. Dorado
    Mixed Technique on Canvas
    760mm x 760mm 2006

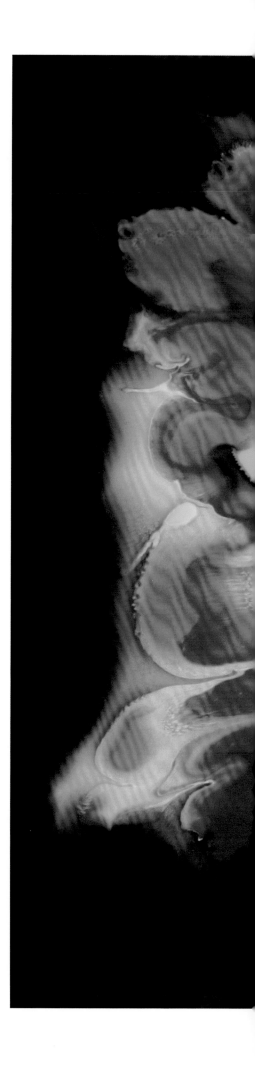

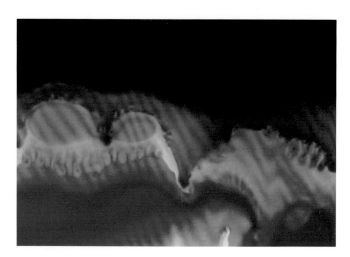

59. Solar Prominence detail

60. Solar Prominence detail

61. Solar Prominence
    Mixed Technique on Canvas
    760mm x 760mm 2006

62

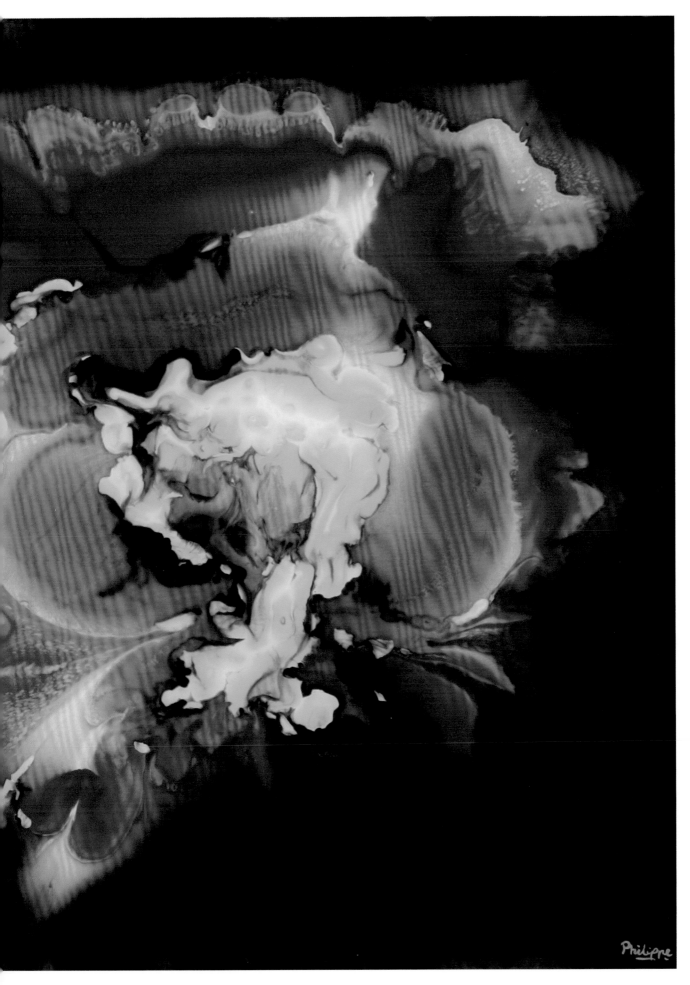

Philippe

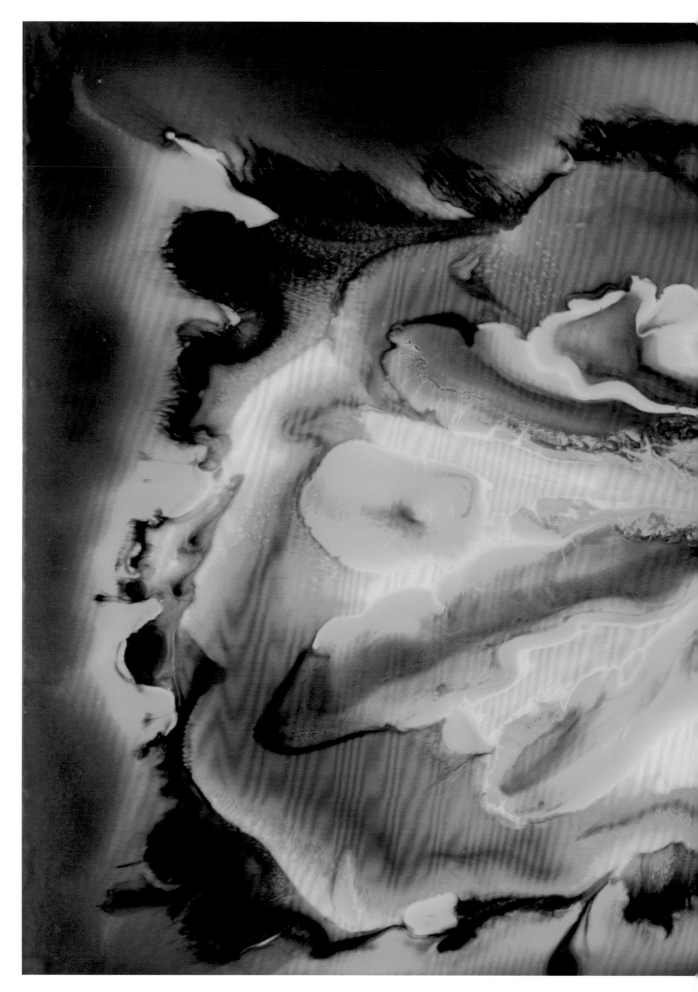

62. Octanus (previous page)
    Mixed Technique on Canvas
    760mm x 760mm 2006

63. Dianthus
    Mixed Technique on Canvas
    760mm x 760mm 2006

64. Dianthus detail

65. Muse
    Mixed Technique on Canvas
    760mm x 760mm 2006

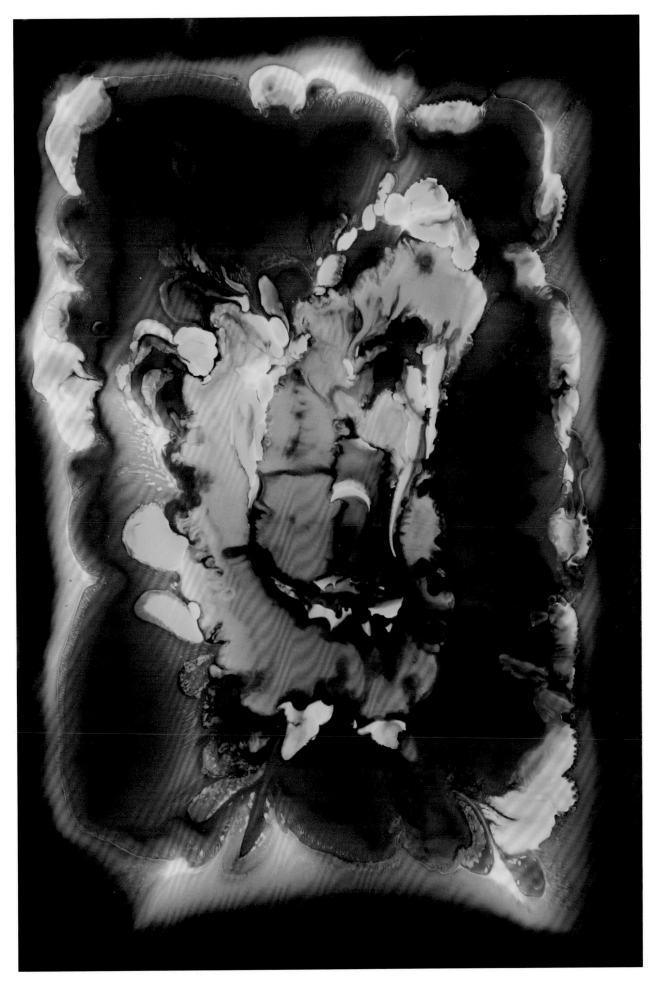

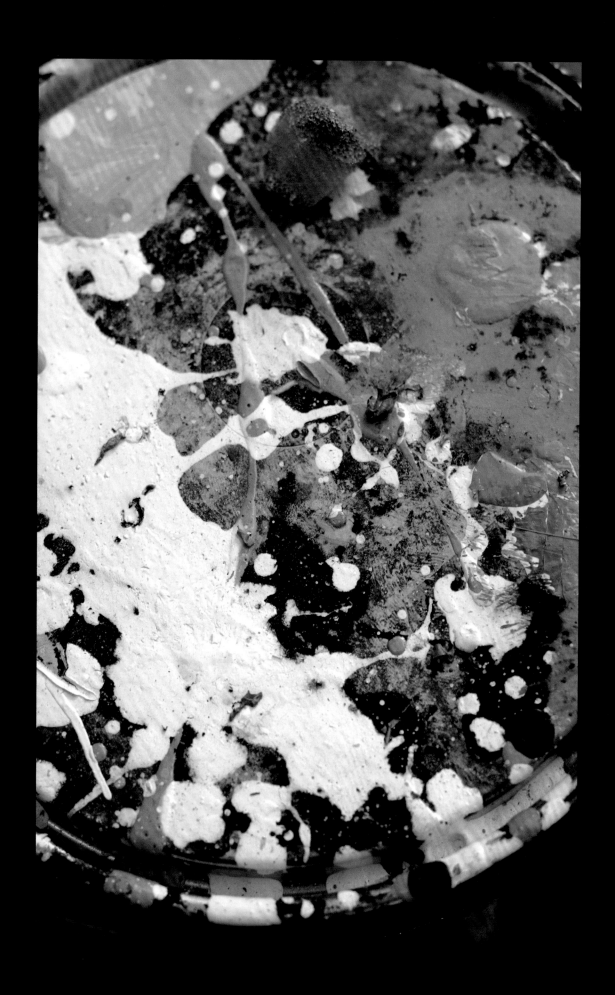

6 FRIENDS AND ALLIES

Generally speaking, people tend to associate with like-minded individuals, and artists are no exception. It is not surprising then, that several of Phil's closest friends share some of his views on art. He has collaborated many times with other artists and the atmosphere at Phoenix reflects his openness to new ideas and lack of competitiveness when it comes to other people's work. His belief in giving artists the freedom to find their own paths is not just some idealized notion - it is a fact, evidenced by a number of friends and allies who have benefited from Phil's generosity. At the same time however, he doesn't suffer fools or time-wasters gladly. Those who don't seem willing or motivated to 'put in the hours' (that phrase again!), are unlikely to receive sustained encouragement. But that's their choice, and there are no hard feelings.

In many ways Phillipe Aird is still a teacher. His approach to it is to ask a student what he/she wants to do and then to help them achieve it by providing terse but relevant comments when necessary. He isn't judgmental, only encouraging. That's not to say he won't criticize - everything he says as a teacher is a critique - but he manages to couch his comments in vocabulary which builds confidence, particularly in young artists or those turning to painting for the first time.

So even after having retired from formal teaching at around thirty, Phil continues to both inspire and encourage others. Among the many budding artists Phil has helped, either overtly or otherwise are Carla Rademan and Masako Sakurai. Carla has been given space and time to turn her ideas into concrete images, both on canvas and in 3-D. A nurse through formal training and currently a florist, Masako's work is still at an early stage but is already attracting interest at Phoenix and elsewhere. Both artists sold their first pieces at Phoenix, and Phil seems almost as proud of that as he is about his own success.

Being willing to take risks, destroy what has been created and then see what transpires as a result is one of the keys, in Phil's eyes, to fulfiling potential.
He is incredibly generous with his time and yet values it dearly. This means that he is very quick to judge whether or not someone is making a serious effort or just waiting to be told (or taught) what to do.
Soon after he opened (and then re-launched) Phoenix, photographer Colin O'Brien happened to drop by looking for some art for his house. The atmosphere and Phil's 'soft-sell' style appealed to him immediately and he returned with his wife and

66. Philippe outside the Phoenix Gallery 2006

bought four paintings. Encouraged by Phil, he began to develop his already considerable photography skills and eventually got into giclé art - photographic printing onto canvas. The results can be seen at Phoenix, and provide another example of Phil's largesse.

In the case of this writer, the dabblings in collage which Phil inspired were quickly replaced when I realized my talents and patience were limited and that my time would be better spent writing about an artist rather than trying to be one!

67. Philippe on the Phone at Phoenix

However, people who meet Phil, particularly at Phoenix, are often inspired in other ways which are not directly connected to painting, or even art in general. He is instinctively wary of 'paralysis by analysis' - the constant need we have to verbalise and dissect our feelings and attitudes in words, theories, frameworks and narrative. To Phil, every picture paints an infinite number of stories, which is why they are superior to and longer-lasting than many a written word. The cave dwelling images at Lascaux in France, for example, tell us as much about that society than any 'learned' text. This is because they are interpretable in many ways, whereas an analysis of them simply gives us one writer's view. Even a photograph of them is still only a photograph.

68. Philippe's sketchbook 2006

69. Philippe's sketchbook 2006

70

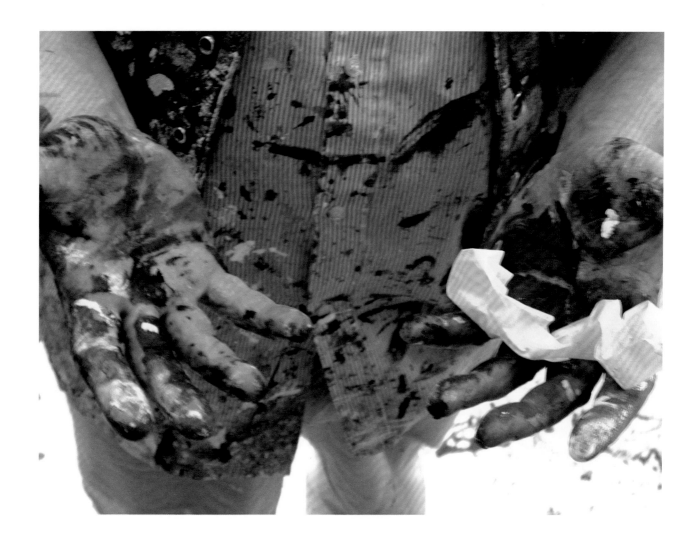

With the possible exception of George Naseby thirty or so years ago, Stephen Flaherty is Phil's biggest collector, having purchased many pieces since meeting him in 1990. Introduced to Phil through George Aird, he has been an art collector since the mid-1970s, and he not only knows what likes, he knows more than a bit about what sells. He was so struck by the quality and uniqueness of Phil's work that he even bought an 'unfinished' canvas straight off the easel! Other than the fact that he thinks the paintings are good, he doesn't see any clear pattern in Phil's work:

'Phil's work has evolved immensely. When I first met him he was doing very good figurative work. It gradually became more abstract, then he started the 'spinning' phase, then more pastel-based, mainly square 'geometric' paintings, and now it's completely different again.'

70. Philippe at work

He suggests that Phil is not governed by the sale-ability of his work but by his desire to explore an ideas or technique until he has mastered it or got bored. *'Whether it sells or not is largely irrelevant to him'*, he says. He describes Phil's current work as gaudy but more powerful - an interesting juxtaposition of adjectives. He also comments that Phil's use of green in several

71. Phoenix Gallery Studio 2006

72

of his most recent pieces makes it unusual. *'You don't see much green in modern art, maybe because it's difficult to place in context'*, he says. As with many people who buy Phil's paintings, he remains enthusiastic about the work and is always curious as to what he'll come up with next. He recently bought a piece for his son, whose age and taste, he feels, are more in keeping with Phil's current output.

'The current work is, to me, more appropriate for commercial spaces, such as offices and large rooms. They dominate their surroundings and need space around them to be at their most effective'.

It's true that the work challenges us more than would traditional landscapes or portraits. They make more of a 'statement' in that they tend to jump out of their surroundings rather than blend in. Mark Fenely at Novus Gallery in south Manchester has seen many a passer-by stop, look and be tempted through the door by the sheer 'in your face-ness' of the work. He is one of many who are genuinely excited by the art but also impressed by the artist himself. *"His view of the world, as expressed through his paintings and his approaches to it, is a truly unique one"*. Phil manages to be modest and very confident at the same time - no mean feat in an artistic environment in which sensationalism, artifice and fashion are often rewarded ahead of care, intellect and intuition.

72. Philippe's sketchbook 2006

73. Polaris 2006 Mixed Technique on Canvas 1750mm x 1000mm

74

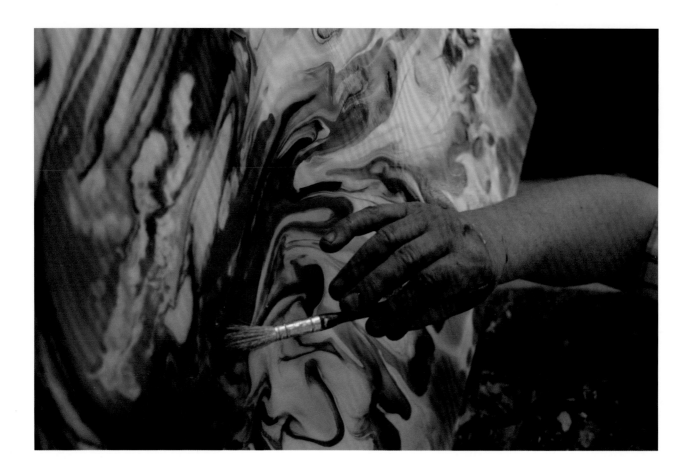

This reaction is echoed by Carla Rademann, who recalls her first impressions of Phil and Phoenix:

74. Philippe at work 2006

"We pulled up to an old warehouse in Hulme, two large, metal doors opened and revealed an incredible Art studio/Gallery, an Aladdin's Cave of art materials. When I think of Philippe, I hear him whistling as he carries a wet canvas over his head from one room to the next. He seems to be totally unaware of the truly beautiful piece of art that he has just created. I see a man covered in paint with knee pads on (he spends a lot of time on the floor!) waltzing through the studio, busy with something that smells very chemical and highly poisonous, but never too busy to take a break to have a smoke and some coffee and feed Sparky (the pigeon)."

Carla continues to explain that Phil has many friends who visit him on a regular basis, several of whom try their hand at painting. But she maintains that *'the only real painting is done by Phil, the rest of us sit around the table in the front waiting for inspiration and discussing new ideas over some coffee'.*

75. The Eye detail 2005
1000mm x 1000mm

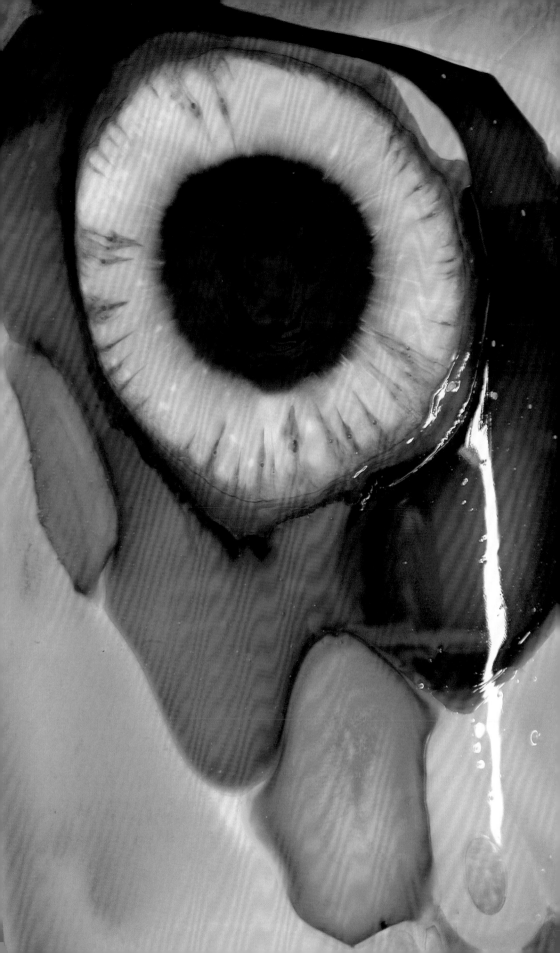

Art Talk

In the summer of 2006 art critic Tom Lubbock wrote, "It's never just liking or not liking (a piece of art). It's about establishing a decisive difference between art that is right and proper and worthwhile and art that is worthless, that is possibly not really art at all".

He goes on to suggest that the lines between the two (right and proper art and the worthless stuff) have become even more blurred over the last twenty years or so, and admits that this has made life more difficult for himself and other critics to go against the grain of populism and try to re-establish some kind of artistic order based on quality rather than the vagaries of the day.

Phil's total immersion in his work might provide such critics with a welcome and refreshing change from the hyper-world of art which tends to vortex itself in places such as London and New York. It might also reassure him that contemporary abstract art continues to be alive and kicking north of Watford!

'Running on self-will is a dangerous path', says Phil. Running on free-will, or 'living in the moment' demands an acceptance of the way things are and the ability to use the existing energy as a force to create something worthwhile. Self-will, in contrast, demands that the energy is directed at achieving or obtaining something from outside the self. Therefore it is ultimately selfish and so restricts the range of possibilities. He also makes the observation that, *'Premeditated things have to adaptable, otherwise they're staged.'*

Staging something implies artificiality. Premeditation implies intent - so the sketch is there already, but the details (where the devil lies) are variable. So we return to Chaos Theory. The variables, irrespective of the overall context - the exact, initial conditions, govern everything. The list of variables governing Phil's work is impossible to identify, and the work may veer off on a different course at any time. One thing is for sure, complacency or predictability will not set in.

Phil is puzzled as to why people are so interested in artists' lives. Perhaps only non-artists can answer this, so I'll make an attempt. Part of the reason seems to be that most of us have dabbled in painting or drawing, even if only as children, so there is a natural curiosity about those for whom it is a full-time occupation. Then there's the romantic notion of the artist creatively daubing away, oblivious to the material cares of the world and the irritants that clutter many peoples' lives. This, largely mythical, idea is difficult to dispel. Thirdly, just as we might want to know something about a favourite musician or footballer - be they commercially successful or not - finding out about what makes

76. Philippe's sketchbook 2006

77. Philippe's shoes 2006

an artist do what he/she does, or the lifestyle he/she leads is part of our culture. The fact that Van Gogh cut his ear off could, theoretically, be completely unrelated to his work. It's unlikely though…

So we seek additional meaning for the painting through the life of the artist. Maybe this is a mistake, but the art and the artist are not easily separable. This is why we're shocked when an artist 'betrays' our perception and 'disappoints' us in some weird way.

So this all begs the question, does it matter if Phillipe Aird has eggs and bacon for breakfast and is partial to custard cream cakes and Capitol Gold radio station? It's like the paintings - if you like them, then that's it, and if you're interested in the person who did them, then you're interested. But this is a mystery to Phil, maybe because he had a unique insight into an artist at such an early age and grew up being familiar with and comfortable in an atmosphere of creative acceptance.

Phil sees his art as his job, saying, *'Nobody asks me to paint these pictures'.*

That's why he isn't overly concerned with the monetary aspect of his work. Of course, he needs the wherewithal to buy the materials to keep on working (and to eat!), and his particularly prolific recent output requires considerable financial outlay. But his favourite painting is always the same - it's the one freshly-stretched canvas lying in his studio waiting to be transformed.

Meditation?

While compiling this book, observing Phil at work and in a variety of situations (albeit mostly within the artistic ecosystem that is Phoenix Studio), I couldn't help asking myself whether or not Phil meditates while painting. This seems unlikely given the physical exertion involved, but perhaps in the moment the paint hits the canvas, like a Japanese calligrapher, there is a kind of release which allows the energy to flow. In sumo, the 'tachi-ai' or moment at which the bout begins, is said to be Zen-like in its significance. This can be seen in Phil's work. Quite how he manages to freeze the moment in such a unique way is a mystery.

But let's get back to basics. Why do people buy Phil's paintings? 'Because they like them' is the most facile answer. And the truest. The work doesn't seek validation, it's a simple 'yes' 'no' thing. A request for an opinion. The whys and wherefores, though interesting, are essentially irrelevant for many of the people who buy his work. This is where the art critic meets his or her match. Based on intellect and paralysis by analysis, the critic is forced to make judgments based on some overarching theory of what constitutes 'good', or indeed 'great' art. It seems clear that when faced with actually buying a painting rather than simply looking at one in a gallery, most people can distinguish between serious attempts at art from *'crowd-pleasing tat'*, as Lubbock terms it. But the unexplained response is also pure, visceral and, like Phil, of the moment. Although he'd prefer you to like his paintings, he's not particularly bothered if you don't. In short, if you think one of Phil's paintings would look good on your wall, then you are right, regardless of the opinions of others. If it is also validated by the approval of those with a reputation for talking of commenting sensibly on art, then so much the better.

This is connected to the relationship between art and society. If, in the end, all art is a matter of opinion, then everyone's view is equally valid, i.e. everyone's a critic. Taken only in the context of 'serious' art criticism, this is almost blasphemy. But if a critic really thinks that the view of a person who has bought a painting of Phil's based on a gut response has less value simply because that person is not an expert, then the arrogance inherent in that view will one day trip itself up. Phil himself is sometimes quite disdainful of 'time-wasters' - those whose main purpose is to show off rather than put in the hours and produce something worthwhile.

But if Phil's paintings speak to you, then that's a fact which no amount of criticism (be it positive or negative) can alter. If they don't, the same holds true. The very fact that you are reading this means that the images in this book have sparked some reaction. But we're getting a bit deep here, and while - generally speaking - deep waters are interesting, most life on earth exists above them.

78. Yohkoh
   Mixed Technique on canvas 2006
   800mm x 1750mm

7 EVOLUTION PHIL AIRD NOW

'Looking back, the major factor in creating my paintings is the necessity of boredom.'

The freedom apparent in Phil's paintings is generated, in part, by the results of acute observation. As well as observing people, Phil sees the relationships between microbiology and cosmology. He also sees connections between the Big Bang and nanotechnology and between the pigeons pottering around outside Phoenix and the ninety paintings which grew legs and wings and flew out of the door in 2003. Of course, he also sees the relationships between his previous work and his current work - and, crucially, the possibilities for the next stage in his artistic evolution. It's not a plan, though.

Several so-called 'northern' artists have been compared and contrasted with the celebrated industrial landscape artist L.S. Lowry. Some welcome it and others don't, but comparisons are inevitable in all forms of expression, be it literature, politics or football. However, in the end anyone can say 'I like it' or 'that's not my cup of tea', or whatever - the personal response is infinitely more important than the critical one. Moreover, the 'informed' response is not automatically superior.

The reasons for mentioning Lowry, given Phil's background, should be clear enough by now, but on the face of it Phil's work could hardly be more different. The similarity between the two artists however, runs deeper than what we choose to see on the canvas. It is to do with a shared sensibility concerning interactions with ordinary people. Lowry achieved this directly through his depictions of working class folk. Phil achieves it by successfully bridging the gap between abstract art and those who previously might have considered it 'not for them'. In another sense though, he is as preoccupied with location as Lowry was, and though the move to Phoenix was largely a matter of convenience, his standard question to visitors to Phoenix isn't even related to the paintings. It's 'How did you find this place, then?'

His studio/gallery isn't exactly in funky downtown Manchester, but the area is one several benefiting from the massive urban regeneration taking place in several parts of the city. However, his work, particularly the abstract stuff, isn't directly related to his working environment, i.e. he isn't merely painting the changes he sees around him; at least not on the surface. It is intuitive and very much of the moment. He follows his heart, his head and his stomach simultaneously.

Art galleries and opening exhibitions are not his favourite ways of spending time - to say the least. Having said that, he is extremely sociable when not working, but even this is largely confined to the self-contained world of his studio. When an idea takes him he's off with the mixer and often produces masses of work in a very short period. For example, he is only (at the time of writing) about six months into his latest series of experiments but this has already yielded over 200 pieces, some of them major works found between these pages.

To 'like' - as opposed to critically appreciate - an artist's work is the simplest and clearest indication of their value to Phil. If you don't like his work he's not particularly offended, but at the same time he won't be sitting down for hour-long conversations about how you think it should be!

In short, Steve Biko's book 'I Write What I Like' is echoed in Phil's attitude to what he does. He works completely intuitively, spewing out the work from within, preferring not to sell new paintings for a while until he can himself absorb their impact. This may sound somewhat random, and it is to a degree. It's like the bloke said of the situation in Northern Ireland not so long ago *'If you're not confused you can't understand it'*. Phil believes that confusion is a healthy state of mind. It is a state in which things can happen and progress be made.

Perhaps an understanding of Phil's work depends on your interpretation of free will and self will. The work is a conscious choice, but he is not driven by the need for the approval of others, and eschews those who have the cheek to 'judge' his work. In other words, it's not an ego trip.

The exhibition which inadvertently provided the target date for completion of this book was curated by Caroline Farmilo and Francesca Fiumano at the Farmilo Fiumano Gallery in London, who have been interested in Phil's work for well over ten years. At Phil's last show there, in 1999, the thoroughfare was temporarily blocked off while a member of the royal family went to have her hair done at the salon opposite, but he's not the type to hold a grudge.

Phil says he's afraid to think too far ahead because he knows that if you want to make God laugh, you just have to tell him your plans. He has also seen several people close to him die at relatively young ages and so is cautious about taking anything for granted. Maybe this goes some way to explaining his urge to be 'of the moment' in his work. We all do things on impulse sometimes, whereas Phil more or less lives on impulse, with regular ingestions of coffee, Sainsbury's strawberry sponge cake, biscuits and the occasional orange. Oh, yes, and the painkillers he takes to soothe the gnawing pain which the physical exertion required by his work entails.

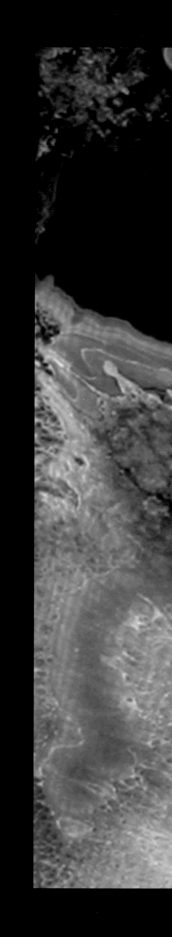

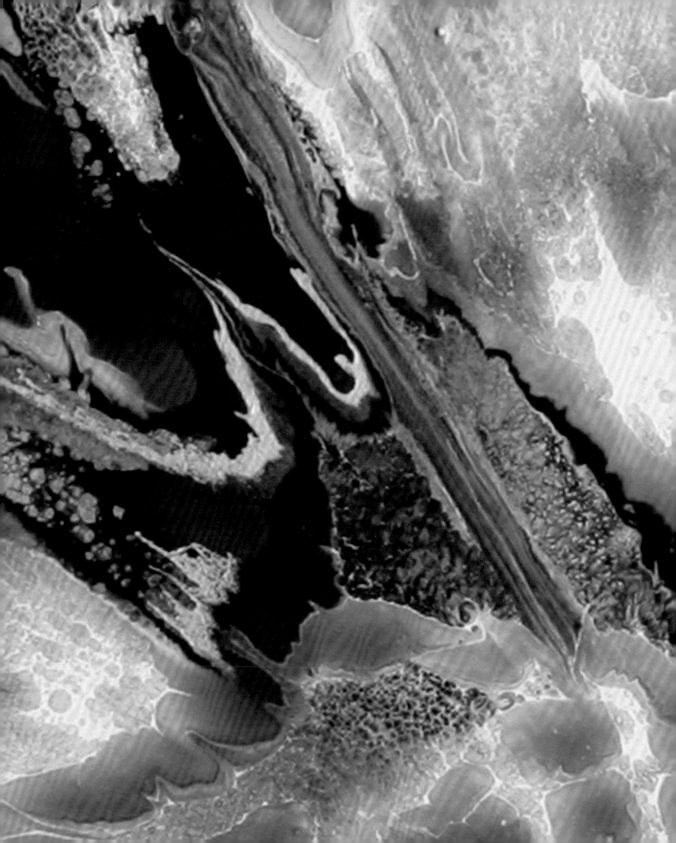

79. Whirlwind Galaxy (previous page) Mixed Technique on canvas 2006 800mm x 800mm

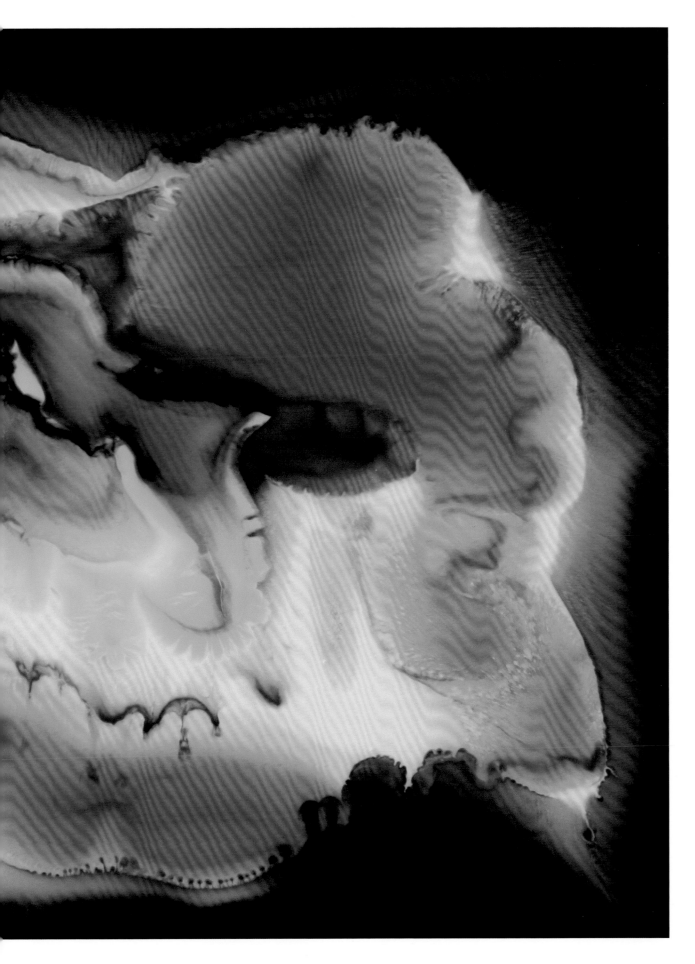

80. Tarantula Nebula 2006 Mixed Technique on canvas 900mm x 600mm

The lure of London notwithstanding, Phil is happy to entrust the nuts and bolts of exhibiting and selling his work to others, as is the case with most other artists. Though his judgment of character is extremely shrewd, he has been ripped off several times - the theft of the paintings in 2003 being only the most dramatic example. It seems he almost sees this as going with the territory, but it is clear that he is hurt by the fact that some are willing to abuse his good nature.

Both individuals and companies have been known to give very strong verbal undertakings to buy large numbers of paintings to adorn their plush offices or investment properties. After many phone calls and emails it emerged that their intentions were two fold;

a) to get the paintings at knock down prices - free if possible, and b) to be seen to make some kind of 'contribution' to the struggling artist.

However, in all such cases, while all the nonsense was flying around, Phil was actually working, packing up the paintings, making arrangements for delivery, and most importantly, producing several new works according to their stated requirements. Such sagas tend to drag on interminably, and Phil's patience is extraordinary. Gradually though, and naturally enough, his patience wears thin - particularly when the paintings are taking up studio space which could be more productively used.

For the moment at least, travel isn't high on Phil's list of particularly worthwhile things to do; though this may change on a whim. A trip to Lytham in early 2006 illustrates this point. On a rare day away from Phoenix (though he'd popped in for two or three hours painting before leaving around 10 o'clock), Phil enjoyed a change of backdrop, the empty or partially filled

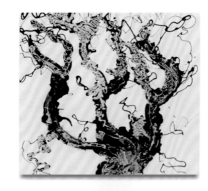

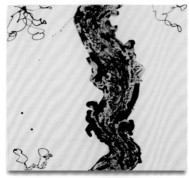

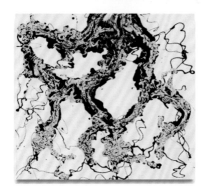

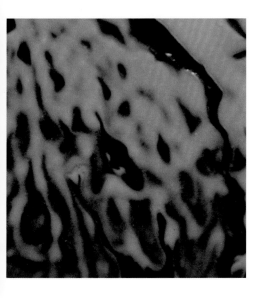

81. Tree detail 2005

82. Tree Triptych 2005

83. Masako and Phil at the Phoenix
Studio 2006

84. Masako and Phil at the Phoenix
Studio 2006

canvases lying forlornly around the studio wondering when their master would be back. Outside several people came and went, their curiosity aroused by the hand-painted signage and photos of the work decorating the doorway. Some may been disappointed, having made a special visit. Others may have simply been mooching around the neighbourhood. Whatever. As chaos theory dictates, they found something else to do with their time which has changed their lives and those of anyone (and anything) else they've interacted with.

The butterflies flapping their wings around new urban Manchester will probably be back - and if not there's plenty more where they came from. The whole issue of sensitive dependence on initial conditions lies at the heart of Phil's work. If the conditions alter slightly, the end result is likely to be massively different - even with the same basic ingredients and environment. The work he would have done had he not gone to Lytham, be it stretching canvases, painting, or feeding the pigeons (which he considers more of a moral responsibility than a job), would have changed things - not only for him but for a mind-boggling collection of others. As it was, he went, and the same holds true. Is this the same for everybody? No idea. Is it 'more true' for some than others? Definitely.
Phil went to Lytham because he felt like it. This is freedom. To do what you want to do. It's not a 'right', so there are no 'responsibilities'.

Having known Phil for only a few months, the task of writing about the paintings and the man is, arguably, easier than if I'd known him longer. In terms of reflecting the work and setting them in some kind of context, this book is the base camp and it's for others to reach the summit. I doubt they'll make it though - as the view from where Phil is would scare most people to death.

Setting Philippe Aird's work within wider contexts of 'northern', 'British', or even 'abstract' art is somehow missing the point. Take the painting which appeared on the cover of 'Urban Life' magazine in mid-2006. The recognizable, definable real-world object which this painting most closely resembles is a dog. Or an upside down dog. Or one doing a handstand. Whatever. Perhaps it's the eye that does it. But Phil did not set out one morning with the intention (premeditation again...) of painting a poodle, any more than the elements intentionally combine to make a cloud look like a giraffe. Of course, the cloud has been transmogrified into something else, but the point is that it was never really a giraffe in the first place. Just as the poodle isn't a poodle. Or a pipe.
The surrealist aspects of the work cannot be underestimated. People from all walks of life see a variety of patterns and connections in Phil's paintings, and simply blurt out their

89

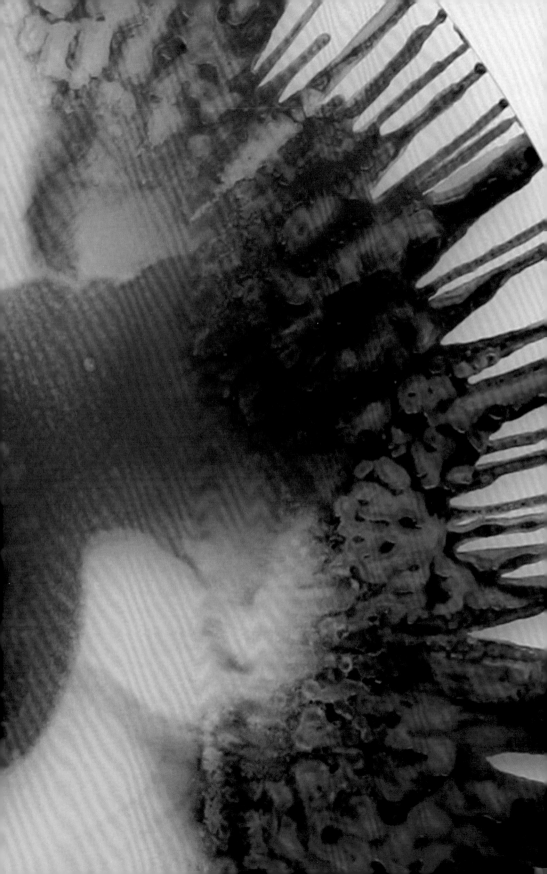

interpretations. *'The Eye'* is perhaps the best example of this and shows how Phil's technique, imagination, and ability to work 'in the moment' blend to produce an image which cannot fail to catch the instant of creation.

Phils work has been described in terms ranging from 'stunningly original' to 'visual puke', each observation as valid as the next. After all, if you think one of his smaller paintings looks like something deposited on a two in the morning pavement, then you're right. Any interpretation inevitably says more about the observer than the originator.

'There are two days that don't belong to us - yesterday and tomorrow'.

This seems to reflect Phil's relationship to his work. It is completely intuitive and he consciously tries to avoid repeating himself or planning too far ahead. If we reduce the statement we eventually arrive at intuition - painting without thinking. If we expand it - a la Matisse - then we have an artistic career plan which, providing genius is present, has more than a snowball's chance in hell of achieving fruition.

The chaos theme is an inescapable part of what Phil produces. But so is functionality. The fact that he puts together the basics of his art - or should we say trade; the wood becomes the frame, the cloth becomes the canvas, the dust becomes the paint - is crucial to understanding the paintings he produces. When he is 'in the moment', he is more organized than the production line at Henry T Ford's factory - the difference being that while Ford prided himself on mass production, Phil prides himself on individuality. Ironic, then, that the very shell in which he works was the site of the mass output of hundreds of different products during Manchester and Salford's industrial (rather than cultural) heyday. This irony is counterbalanced by his empathy with the former workers in those mills. He doesn't identify so much with the products, but with the people who made them. As did Lowry.

Phil's working method is constantly evolving because of his intense practice of using new mediums to create beautiful tactile surface. The process is intense and physically challenging.

Caroline Farmilo says, *"I consider Philippe Aird to be a contemporary artist more in harmony with Turner than, say, Damien Hirst"*. This is a telling observation, because it places Phil's work firmly within nature, which the artist himself acknowledges as the source of all original beauty. Phil is chasing the origins of our universe, but not blindly. His curiosity is unending, and his unerring eye continues to find new forms of expression.

85. Solar II 2005 800mm x 800mm

A Conversation with Philippe Aird

Phoenix Gallery, 8th August 2006.
As part of the preparation for this book, friend and fellow-artist James Bloomfield talked to Philippe about his art.
Below are some salient excerpts:

JB: Have you ever had a desire to be a figurative painter?

PA: No, because I've always been a figurative painter, I've always painted figuratively. Its just recently, the last sort of two, no, three years gone abstract. But having said that, in some ways they're more figurative anyway because the viewer starts reading in all these figurative responses, whether its faces, animals, objects, fish, whatever, and also they're from space you know, the explosions, which is abstract in itself. But they're just like anything else is, and images from the body. The book I studied on the body appears to be abstract, so it's a funny mix-up. But also the abstract allows me to experiment more.

JB: You began doing figurative paintings, exploring different forms within those parameters. Do you think you've 'been there/done that', or is it something you've decided to leave for the moment and this is where your at now?

PA: Yes. This is where I am at the moment, but I certainly don't think I've done it as in the figurative aspect, also there are just so many figurative images when you're driving, moving, you're just bombarded with figuration, and also the distortion of figuration, through, you know, computers and stuff, for me it's more perplexing to a degree for the viewer; abstraction, maybe? It allows them greater freedom to read what the hell they want into them, I'm still reluctant to title them, so that freedom they have, they can start to impose their own interpretation on it. Whereas with a portrait of someone's head, it's someone's head, do I recognize who it is, right? That's it, too a degree.

JB: Then you must enjoy painting this way; it must be freedom for you in a way?

PA: Yes, I'm not anchored down by the err, the figurative aspect that would hold me back, and also one's often subservient to it. If you had a model it's such a powerful thing, whether they're clothed or not clothed, you'll have somebody in a room, for me its difficult enough to paint when there's a spider, let alone if somebody's there, or even still life, anything, you're subservient.

The thing I've decided to look in is myself, into my stomach. As apposed to looking out and you then gather information, and then you recycle it. It was a different procedure.

JB: I've never thought of it in that kind of way.

PA: It's right for me.

JB: So with this process you're exploring materials and ideas at the moment, so you're not subservient to any a subject matter as such. Would you say you're limiting yourself to exploring materials rather than subject matter?

PA: Not limiting, because that's the thing that keeps me going and excited. It's trying to come across new sorts of materials, new techniques and that takes, like these paintings here that are on show, you know they've taken me 15 years to suss out the technique of trial and error, and you lose confidence. When everything doesn't work, try this leave it you know, there's something a gut, you know an instinct, you're trying to express, you don't know at the time, but when I know I've achieved it you get bored with it. I want the next thing. There's so many unusual materials now on the market, different things, that I'm always out looking for something a bit peculiar, you never know what you get. As apposed to going to an art shop, you tend to get art materials, don't you?

JB: So other artists are limited by their materials in that they generally only source them from one place, which is a more traditional approach - something you're working to free yourself from….

Pause

JB: I know you've destroyed a lot of your paintings in the past, I've seen them in the skip. Is that part of it? Do you think there's no great shame in doing something and admitting that it's not worked out and chucking it away?

PA: No, and in a way they're the best ones It was the same with snooker - I used to like losing to a degree, because I'd learn more, not all the time of course, you lose confidence. But in a way they're the best ones because they're the ones I've learnt through - they're the crucial stepping stones to the ones you see on the wall and the ones I've sold. To get there you could argue, as with Jackson Pollock's really early work, how he got there was far more interesting than what he arrived at. Once he'd got there he was drippy drippy, like mad you know, one after the other. But the process of getting there was actually far more revealing,

93

exciting and experimental. It makes we wonder why and how he carried on in that manner, you know? I'm sure he got bored.

JB: You get into that comfort zone, if you get something that works, and you're getting praise for things, for the way they look, you kind of get tied to it. Maybe a lot of artists think 'well, this is me, this is what I do so I'm going to keep doing this because this is obviously what I'm going to become famous for'.

PA: Well, you've got to pay the bills, make a living, but you can't get out of your own skin - it's still going to be you by experimenting, and then you're still going on a journey, you're setting sail each time, you're exploring, you know? This is the drive, the quest for mastery - or as close as you can get. Yes, I've completed all these paintings, but there's also lots and lots of other things that I just haven't done and will never do, which turns me on in a way. I just keep trying to move forward through experimentation.

JB: Looking back through art history, do you think abstract painting still has a place out there? The great abstract painters like Rothko, I know you've mentioned Pollock and all those abstract expressionists, in the era from the 1950s through to the 60s, they were giants. And then it all seemed to stop. The art world declared the new thing was 'installation art' or someone else was the new future, or 'this is where art should be now'. Does that bother you or do you not really give a monkeys?

PA: I think it's a load of nonsense myself, so no, I don't give a monkeys. For me, the first sort of abstract images were and still are to be found in nature. Whether it be space, which is the obvious one for me, or on the body, the inside of the body, but also in rock formations, stratification, the patterns and shapes you see when you look closely at certain trees, the bark, the insides. They're abstract images in a way, especially when you focus in on an area, just as an artist does, it picks out a particular composition, if you move in, it will always be far superior to anything a human mind or hand can achieve. As for new art forms or fashion, then I'm just not the slightest bit concerned with it - it's so transient I just couldn't give a damn.

86. The Phoenix Gallery 2005

JB: You've said before over analysis leads to paralysis. Could you expand on that?

87. Vaporum Mixed technique on canvas 800mm x 1700mm 2006 Private Collection

PA: There was a student in last week who told me that drawing was coming back into colleges, which to tell you the truth, having taught for seven years and heard different things every year about this being the new thing or whatever, it was such a, I don't know if the word is parochial or insular, but about the only people that bloody care are the artists anyway. And then there's real fashion that's governed by certain people, it just changes from year to year or every two years or something. For me it's the integrity of the work and the individual that's of real, lasting importance - whatever he or she wishes to express their emotions through shape, colour, writing, whatever it might be, then as long as the bloody stuff's good it's OK. And contains an echo of their chemicals, an echo of them. As apposed to being some sort of pretentious superficial thingy dingy.

JB: So it doesn't matter how someone expresses themselves as long as it's an honest expression of what they wanted to say?

PA: As long as it's not violent, or inciting violence or any flipping political thingy dingy.

JB: So you don't do that 'fundamentalist Catholics at school' and all that kind of sensationalist stuff?

PA: No, it's not for me. But it is a spiritual journey without a doubt, but it would lead me to, wherever it's bloody leading me to, mainly by being honest with the materials, to follow the colour to follow the shape, to follow the chance. It's taken years

88. Phoenix studio 2006

89. Phoenix studio 2006

really, of breaking down all the logical nonsense and then being able to follow the messages, the signs. This for me is very spiritual indeed, especially living in the moment when you're doing it, it just directs me and it also breeds ideas up, I'll try this or I'll try that. So it has to be intuitive really, instinctive…. it feels like, as if something else is in control at times, I don't know what it is...

JB: That's what a lot of painters claim to be after. That childlike zone, forgetting everything that you've ever been taught, or shown, or seen or conditioned into. It seems that at the moment your life is structured around being in that place as much as possible.

PA: I think it is, well, it is. I'm here every day and I have to put in the time I think because basically I'm not very good. Whereby I have to keep an eye on things, I have to, it's almost like some sort of very thin thread and once its broken a little bit it takes weeks to rebuild. And a lot of my work is based on rhythm and the flow of adrenalin anyway, so I just have to put in the time and try and be organized for the chaos of when I do paint. Or be prepared for the complete freedom of when I paint.

JB: Is there a particular part of the day where you feel you get this more readily?

PA: Yes. Most simply early in the morning, early in the morning I've got a couple of brain cells left, usually until about half nine, half ten, and then its almost a robotic activity - plodding along throughout the day then with half a brain cell. I'm best in the morning, but I never used to be.

JB: I was going to ask, has it always been like that?

PA: No, I just changed one day. I used to lie in bed for ages, which I miss, but now I can't. I just get up and go. But there're two sides to a routine for me you know, I need that routine, I need that structure to keep moving forwards. As I say, there's so many other possibilities to be explored, which keeps me going, but there's also the other side of the coin. I suppose a holiday may help to break up the boredom of locking the doors, the same routine each day, this and that, switch this on, etc, etc, you know, there's also the numbing aspect of the routine as well. But then that's not the biggest burden in the world. Having got to know and seen the builders around here (there's huge rebuilding going on around Phil's studio), most of them going to work each day throughout winter, and working grinding metal, building, banging and all that, I don't think I've got much to complain about. That routine would do me in a bit more.

JB: Do you feel like you're totally inside that routine, or could you quite easily just forget it and go and do something else?

PA: I think all I'm protective over is the creative process, the highs and lows... its all I have in the end, so I'm very protective over that. If I wasn't it'd be very easy to fill my time. For example, last weekend I took Sunday afternoon off and went to this old folk's home which has some paintings of mine. But even that affected me, the different atmosphere, the distraction if you like. The next day I was out of sync for most of the day, just wasn't in tune in the morning, so even that had affected me, but…

JB: Is that because it was throwing something new at you - new ideas or new possibilities or a whole new experience? Did you have to work through it before you could get back into your routine?

PA: I think so, yes. On the way home I had to find the same journey home, get the petrol from the same bloody petrol station. I don't go to exhibitions, I don't go out to get, you know, so called 'inspiration', sketching in the landscape or whatever. It may be I just don't bother, I don't seem to need to, there's so many things in my stomach that I just wish I could bring out, really. The

90. Phil at the Phoenix studio 2006

distractions would lead me somewhere else, but there's more than enough of my own chemicals, my own makeup that I wish to explore, through instinct. In any case, doing a painting is like going on holiday... it takes me to wherever it takes me. So that recharges me. It's like going on a journey each bleedin' time. So in that sense I have holidays throughout the year.

JB: I suppose that really what you've just said is these are all still coming from you, coming out of you, like some mad coral that's continually ejaculating spermatozoa, breeding and throwing out?

PA: Yes. Yes, that's a good analogy. When I was sixteen on my moped, coming from Salford, it was like shapes and colours in my stomach that I just wanted to bring out. I even described it as visual puke. Puking this stream of colours and shapes from within, but this is obviously not a logical process. It's intuitive painting, it's instinctive, so they're subliminal images. There's so much of the sublime - seventy five percent of the head or wherever it is, there's so much for me to tap into there. But if I go out of that door now, there are so many distractions it confuses me. You know, if I'm out for a day or two, or take a week off, I lose that contact with myself because I'm bombarded with all sorts of bloody things. Even a traffic jam affects my rhythm and the adrenalin disappears…

JB: A lot of painters would find that a difficult way to paint.

PA: Well, for me it could be seen as a prison sentence. I'm in here every day - day in day out doing long hours, but again it doesn't matter to me. It's however you do it, you know? Differences among artists in terms how they do it are not important, as long as they do it. For example, a mate of mine, Charlie Shiels is going to bed when I'm getting up, you know he paints until early in the morning, starts late…but that's how he does it …it's each to his own. But any artist for me should be expressing their own make-up, their own particular chemicals. They have to because of the fact that they've done it, and every single person is different, always have been throughout history, millions and millions of people. So it's quite a beautiful thing to express your own… to find out about yourself. And sentencing yourself to this particular journey is err…, well it's fine.

JB: I look at your paintings differently now, they're not trying to stand up against another painting and say 'look at how good I am compared to you', or 'look how I do it compared to how you've done it' - it doesn't matter.

PA: It doesn't.

JB: I think this is good because there are so many artists that have got this boil in their stomach that they want to get out, they want to do something, but they're so constricted, or so scared to do something.

PA: I think I've had some of that for years, but I saw some Korean art and read a bit about it and evidently they see artists as they would see a plumber or a cook - an integral part of society. One of the problems of being an artist in a society is if they try to put themselves - or allow themselves to be put - above other people. You know, this thing where you're an 'artist', which I still don't understand, that people are fascinated by an artist, whereas for me, if I'm like a cook or a plumber or builder, then I put the time in - the hours. And I don't want to be like 'I'm the best builder in the world because I've laid so many bricks' or whatever. But by putting in the time and the hours you know, it's a job! But quite a lovely job, it is a lovely job, because you learn about yourself,

91. Philippe and James Bloomfield
Bloomfieldart Studio 2006

100

exploring and moving forward. But it's a very polluted area without a doubt.

JB: What do you mean by polluted?

PA: It's mainly polluted by the individual. I think there' s a whole structure out there, the way we discuss paintings, that I don't understand, but I think half of it is polluted by the individual.
'I want to be an artist or write a book or do a painting', and the image of all that I think is a very dangerous path! I actually wouldn't mind as long as the time is put in and there's work there to back it up. If the time isn't evident, then it's not an honest reflection, unless it's bloody good!
But that's very easy to say but it's very difficult to sort of find out what you're about anyway and to put the time in as well.
There's also that statement, "Luck is a mess of preparations meeting opportunity". To create your own luck. All that preparation and work and luck will start to come in, that's what I meant about the spiritual thing in the paint directing me. Then chance and luck for me will start to happen. It's like the icing on the cake, but I can't just start hanging out and hoping for a bit of luck to turn up - for me it doesn't happen. So the ingredients start to slot into place and hopefully through that foundation, that boring, solid, monosyllabic base, I can get on with the bloody job! Having said that, I spend two or three days a week cleaning. Ha ha!

JB: That's where you're using all your luck up!

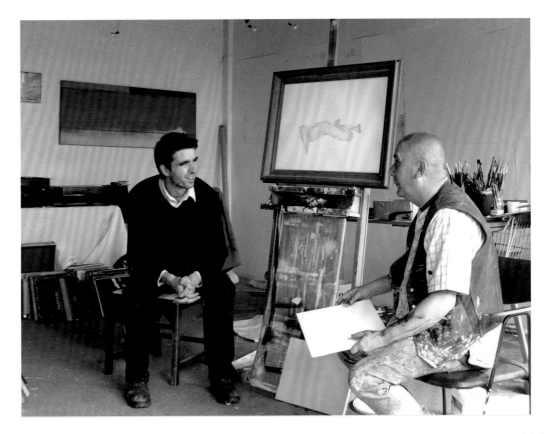

"It is said that Francis Bacon walked into a gallery in London one day, wrote a cheque for a very considerable amount for one of his own paintings, took it outside and destroyed it. In the summer of 2006, as we have seen, a 'collector' of Phil's work was captured on CCTV clambering out of a skip with an unwanted canvas under his arm. This was one of hundreds of paintings which eventually find their way in the world - starting out at Phoenix and contributing to their creator's journey."

Philippe Aird: Chronology

1961   Born 14th July at home next to Cheadle Heath sewerage works.

1967   Attended Cheadle Heath Primary School.

1972   Attended Dialstone Secondary School, Offerton.

1973   Transferred to Broadway Secondary School, Cheadle.

1973   Exhibited at Stockport Art Gallery (School Show).
            Featured in Local then National press for his ability to
            copy old masters, Rembrandt, Carravagio, Cezanne.

1975   Family moved to Cheadle.

1977   Enrolled on an Art Foundation Course at Salford.
            College of Technology to study Fine Art/ Graphic Design Textiles/ Printmaking.

1980   Won scholarship to Chelsea School of Art.

1982   Won the 1st 'Time Out' International Video Festival Award.

1983   Graduated from Chelsea with a B.A. Hons. in Fine Art.
            Began teaching at Salford College of Technology.
            Made a film in Menai Village, Anglesey.

1984   Shared a studio (a former abbatoir in Stockport), with brother André.

1985-87   Worked at a studio in Brixton, London, whilst working as a
            motorcycle courier and as a chef in Chelsea.

1987   Stratford-upon-Avon Show.

1988-89   Taught 4-day Life Class course and 4 evenings at Salford and Stockport.
            Acted in 'Golden Years' at Beatrix Potter's Cottage in the Lake District, UK.

1989   Travel Scholarship to Spain. Studied "Guernica" and the
            working process of the 47 drawings and studies.

1989   Moved into a former fish & chip shop in Stockport, using it as a workshop/studio.

1989   Visited Amsterdam's Van Gogh Museum.

1990   Grants from Salford Arts and Educational Media Trust - travelled to Spain.

1991   Began as a part-time Lecturer at Stockport College.

1991	Travelled round Scotland. Visited Paris and the Louvre.
1992	Featured on BBC "Forty Minutes" Documentary.
1992	Exhibited in San Fransisco.
1992	Exhibited at Edinburgh Film Festival.
1992	Sotherby's Group Show, London.
1993	Travel Scholarship to America.
1992	Won an Eric Simm Travel Scholarship and travelled to Spain, and Ireland. Also went to Paris and Amsterdam.
1996	Travelled to Milan, Venice and Verona.
1997	Metro Show Bury.
1996	Became full time Lecturer at Stockport College.
2003	Opened Phoenix Studio/Gallery in Castlefield, Manchester. Opening night robbery results in the loss of over 90 pieces.
2004	Exhibited at Farmilo Fiumano Gallery, London.
2005	Manchester Art Show at GMEX, MICC.
2005	Featured in 'City Life' Magazine, Manchester.
2006	Leeds Temple Bar Show.
2006	GMEX Show, Manchester.
2006	Featured in 'Concept for Living' & 'Urban Life' magazines.
2006	The Eye' show at Novus Contemporary Art, Manchester.
2006	Featured in the 32nd Edition of 'Who's Who In Art'.
2006	Launch of book 'Eye of the Beholder'.
2006	'Sex Chemistry' show at Farmilo Fiumano Gallery, London.

To enter Phoenix Gallery is to enter Aladdin's cave
Of psychedelic images where forms and textures
rave
A treasury of canvases that stand, hang, lean or lie
And across the waiting surfaces a firestorm roars by
And vivid, vitreous colours explode in a million
flashes
Moving in all directions and streaks and strokes and
slashes
A meteor storm of brushstrokes in glorious free fall
Whirling, swirling spirals, pulsars throbbing on the
wall
And Philippe in his workshop like an alchemist of old
Follows his inspiration in producing pure gold.

Pat Brock